Awaken the Giant

Two Lay Leaders Speak Out

Awaken the Giant

28 Prescriptions for Reviving
The United Methodist Church

James W. Holsinger, Jr.
Evelyn Laycock

200 38
Abingdon Press / Nashville

AWAKEN THE GIANT
28 Prescriptions for Reviving The United Methodist Church

Copyright © 1989 by Abingdon Press

This book is printed on acid-free paper.

Library of Congress Cataloging-in-Publication Data

Holsinger, James W., 1939-
   Awaken the giant: 28 prescriptions for reviving The United Methodist Church/James W. Holsinger, Jr., Evelyn Laycock.
      p. cm.
   Includes index.
ISBN 0-687-02321-1 (alk. paper)
      1. Church renewal—Methodist Church. 2. United Methodist Church (U.S.) 3. Methodist Church—United States. I. Laycock, Evelyn. II. Title.
BX8382.2.H65   1989
262'.0017—dc19   88-37590
                                                                                         CIP

Scripture quotations unless otherwise noted are from the Revised Standard Version of the Bible, copyright 1946, 1952, 1971 by the Division of Christian Education of the National Council of the Churches of Christ in the USA, and used by permission.

Scripture quotations noted NIV are taken from the Holy Bible: New International Version. Copyright © 1973, 1978, 1984 by the International Bible Society. Used by permission of Zondervan Bible Publishers.

The prayer on page 70 by Henry H. Tweedy is quoted from *Consider the Grass . . . God Cares for You,* copyright 1974 by Baker Book House Company. Used by permission.

MANUFACTURED BY THE PARTHENON PRESS AT
NASHVILLE, TENNESSEE, UNITED STATES OF AMERICA

Dedicated to

the church we love
that nurtures us
in the Christian faith

and

to Barbara and Bill
our covenant partners
in life

Contents

Why Should Laypeople Write This Book?

For some time the two of us have spent many hours discussing our beloved church. Over and over again we have spoken of our concern for her, wondering what we could do to bring about the recovery of her greatness. Perhaps it was the bicentennial of American Methodism that called to us. Perhaps it was the knowledge of the historical greatness of Methodism that tugged at our hearts. Perhaps it was the thought that our denomination seemed to have much in common with the Church of England in Wesley's day that caught our attention. In any event, we found ourselves assailed by the thought that something somewhere was amiss with our denomination. So as we worked together on several projects, as we talked together, as we thought together, the idea of writing a book together began to intrude on our collective consciousness. We were aware, of course, of the recent books that have discussed the current state of our church and we noted that they had been written by several bishops and seminary professors. We believed, however, that there was a place for a book written by laypeople, by laypeople who have spent their lives in The United Methodist Church, laypeople who love and believe in The United Methodist Church. So it is to that end that we decided that we would write a book that would set forth plainly our concerns with the current state of The United Methodist Church and we would plainly set forth our prescriptions for her.

Bishop Nolan B. Harmon, some years ago, stated that the laypeople of The United Methodist Church are like a sleeping giant. We believe that should the sleeping giant be awakened The United Methodist Church could once again rise to a position of influence with the American people, winning hearts and souls to Jesus Christ. The laypeople of The United Methodist Church have continued through the years to support her with their prayers, their presence, their gifts, and their service. But somehow, somewhere, they have lost their fire and fervor. Somehow, United Methodist laypeople in the United States have become domesticated. As

Bishop Harmon so aptly put it, they have fallen asleep. We firmly believe that it is time for the laypeople of our denomination to awaken, and once awakened, to move The United Methodist Church into and through her third century with a powerful impact on our society. We propose in this book to discuss a variety of issues. All United Methodists are aware of the decline in membership in our denomination and no book dealing with the state of our denomination can fail to come to grips with this issue. We have great concern for the status and role of our clergy, particularly in light of the past five General Conferences establishing study commissions to look at its possible overhaul. As laypeople ourselves, we are fully aware of the belief of many if not most laypeople that the general agencies of the denomination are simply irrelevant to their life as Christians. Why then has the general church apparently become irrelevant to the people in the pew?

When dealing with theology, particularly in the guise of pluralism, it appears to many laypeople that The United Methodist Church does not have a theology. What is the place of Wesleyan theology in the life of our denomination? As laypeople we are concerned with the place of the local church in the life of United Methodism. Does the local church have a place in the mission of the church, and if so, does it have a role in the connectional system called The United Methodist Church? The question of the character of United Methodism in the United States is an extension of the local church issue. Has our church fully become united following the unions of the past fifty years, or does it remain a group of regional churches or fiefdoms resulting from the unions? In any event does it really matter as far as the laypeople are concerned? In this context, how does a major denomination such as ours function effectively without a clear-cut executive branch of government? Between quadrennial General Conferences, how does The United Methodist Church function, or does it function at a general church level at all? It is our basic premise that United Methodist laypeople are the answer to the future of the denomination. How then can the giant be awakened?

One of our major concerns with the several books written on the state of The United Methodist Church is that they have seemingly failed to explicitly set forth specific suggestions for renewing the denomination. We will close this effort with specific suggestions, "prescriptions," for The United Methodist Church. For it is our deep-seated belief that there is hope for The United Methodist Church! We believe that reports of her coming demise are premature and the third century of The United Methodist Church will be one of lasting influence. Quite simply, we are firmly convinced that there is hope for The United Methodist Church.

We have long been concerned with the apparent silence of United Methodist laypeople. However, we are concerned that perhaps those who wanted to be heard simply took the easy way by voting with their feet. Perhaps those who left have been the most concerned with the direction, or lack thereof, of The United Methodist Church. We believe that the laypeople of our denomination should have the right to be heard. It is for this reason that we have written this book, though we fully acknowledge that we are but two laypeople among millions and that our opinions are our own. In addition, we should clarify that unless otherwise noted, we are talking about The United Methodist Church in the United States. We are calling upon United Methodist laity in the United States to awaken; and it is with the current situation of United Methodism in the United States that this book is particularly concerned.

Perhaps one of the best analogies of our denomination is Jonathan Swift's *Gulliver's Travels*. In this classic story, Gulliver, the "giant" is finally bound tightly by the "little" people while he is asleep. It may just be that, while it has been asleep, our beloved church has been bound by the "little" people—all of us—laypeople, clergy, and bishops alike. It is our firm belief that the time has come for our great church to reawaken to the call of the Risen Lord and become the giant for service and witness that God has called it to be!

CHAPTER 1

Where Are We Today?

"A sower went out to sow. And as he sowed, some seeds fell along the path, and the birds came and devoured them. Other seeds fell on rocky ground, where they had not much soil, and immediately they sprang up, since they had no depth of soil, but when the sun rose they were scorched; and since they had no root they withered away. Other seeds fell on good soil and brought forth grain, some a hundredfold, some sixty, some thirty. He who has ears, let him hear" (Matt. 13:3b-9).

When Jesus taught in parables, and this was his characteristic form of teaching, he was presenting deep eternal truths that form the nature of the universe. In the parable of the sower, Jesus describes four types of soil in which seeds are sown: hard, rocky, thorny, and good. Seeds that fall on the first three soils do not grow because the conditions are such that the life power contained in the seed cannot burst forth and grow toward maturity. However, there is a fourth soil, described as good, which produces harvests of 100 percent, 60 percent, and 30 percent. The harvest figures in the story seem unbelievable to the hearers.

Using seed as a metaphor for the kingdom of God and good soil as any place where the kingdom of God is received, Jesus is saying God's kingdom may be experienced as lived reality *now* and in the *age to come.* This divine rule of God is active in the good soil which may be individuals, churches, or nations. With the kingdom comes all the resources of God for use in the *now.* From this interrelatedness comes a harvest beyond human comprehension.

This eternal truth from God means new life and dynamic growth are possible for The United Methodist Church, for there certainly is no seed shortage; and Jesus said it is God's good pleasure to give the kingdom.

We need then to take a look at how this process can begin. The parable reveals that the soil needs to be examined, for in it is the power of life or death. Therefore, for a new life, strong growth, and great harvests, the place to begin is by asking the question, What kind of soil is The United Methodist Church—rocky, hard, thorny, or good? For in the answer lies the power of life or death!

* * * *

As a denomination, The United Methodist Church has slowly but surely declined in total membership for the past quarter century. The length of the decline establishes the fall in membership as a significant aspect of denominational life. The result is that at the end of 1987 United Methodist Church membership in the United States stood at 9,021,217, a decrease of 70,248 members from the previous year.[1] There are several questions that need to be asked.

Paul Huber, a layman in the Virginia Annual Conference, has carefully looked at the membership figures of The United Methodist Church. In addition to the usual charting of membership in millions of members (Figure 1), he has also looked at the membership of The United Methodist Church as a percent of the total population of the United States (Figure 2). When the basic question, What has happened to the membership of The United Methodist Church? is asked, it is clear that in total members, the denomination reached its peak just prior to the union of The Methodist Church and the Evangelical United Brethren Church in 1968. The 1964 reports of the two denominations listed a combined total membership of 11,054,634.[2] By 1968, the actual year of union, the combined total membership of the new denomination was 10,809,502.[3] As noted by both Warren J. Hartman, formerly executive director of the Office of Research of the General Board of Discipleship, and Paul Huber, the initial decline following union was slow for several years. However, during the next twenty years the loss of members would become a hemorrhage.

A careful review of Figures 1 and 2 is instructive. From 1784 with the founding of the Methodist Episcopal Church in the United States, a steady growth in membership occurred even following the division of the church into the Methodist Protestant Church and the northern and southern divisions of the Methodist Episcopal Church. Following the Civil War, the three denominations continued to grow rapidly in numerical strength until peak membership in 1964. Membership now approximates the denominational membership during the period of World War II.

FIGURE 1

Growth and Decline in Membership of United Methodist Church and Predecessor Bodies

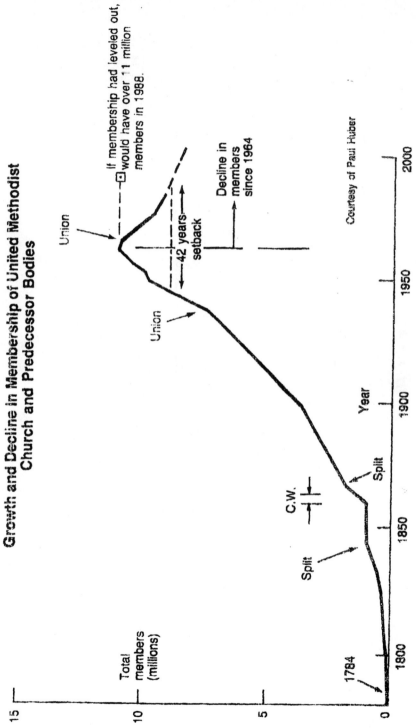

Courtesy of Paul Huber

FIGURE 2
Chronology of Membership

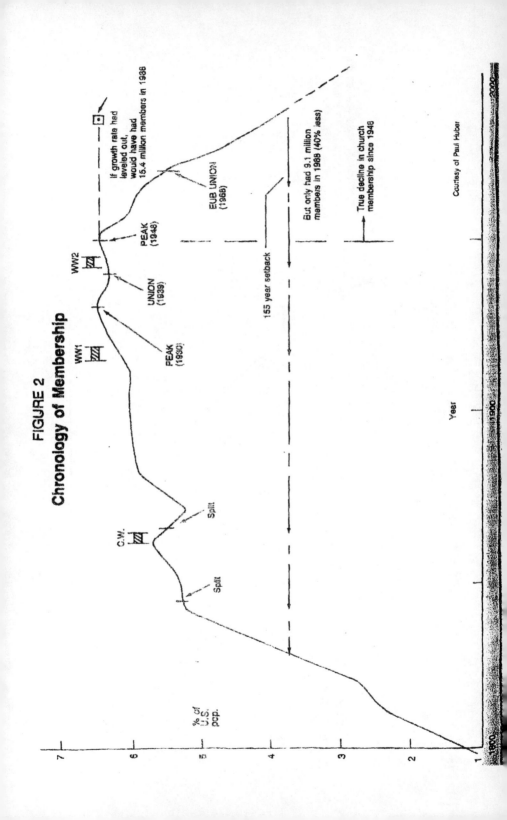

If growth rate had
leveled out,
would have had
15.4 million members in 1936

PEAK
(1948)

WW2

EUB UNION
(1968)

UNION
(1939)

WW1

PEAK
(1930)

But only had 9.1 million
members in 1988 (40% less)

155 year setback

True decline in church
membership since 1948

C.W.

Split

Split

% of
U.S.
pop.

Year

Courtesy of Paul Huber

7

6

5

4

3

2

1

1800   1900   2000

However, Figure 2 more realistically approximates the real situation as membership of The United Methodist Church (or its predecessor denominations) is compared to total United States population as a percentage of the whole. In this mode, the Methodist Episcopal Church reached a total in excess of 5 percent of the U.S. population in 1844 just prior to its division into regional churches. As a percentage of the U.S. population the Methodist Episcopal Church; the Methodist Episcopal Church, South; and the Methodist Protestant Church declined by nearly 40 percent at the beginning of the Civil War. Following the war, these three denominations regained strength reaching nearly 5 percent of the population. The three denominations steadily grew for nearly eighty years, reaching an all time high of nearly 6.5 percent of the U.S. population in 1930 and again in 1948, just nine years following the birth of The Methodist Church in 1939. At this point the denomination entered into a forty-year decline in membership with the 1968 union between The Methodist Church and the Evangelical United Brethren Church not even producing an upward blip in the steadily downward trend. Thus in contradistinction to the normally accepted date of denominational decline of 1964, the actual decline began nearly twenty years earlier. The result of the forty-year period of declining membership has been a reduction of 40 percent in the membership of The United Methodist Church as a percentage of the population of the United States. Had The United Methodist Church maintained its peak percentage of 1948, the denominational membership would stand at 15,400,000 in 1988. The current numerical strength of the denomination represents a level equal to that of 150 years ago, a figure equal to approximately 4 percent of the U.S. population.

With a loss of nearly 40 percent of the denomination's strength as a percent of U.S. population, it is not difficult to recognize the decrease in denominational impact on the structures of the United States. A denomination with a forty-year history of decline is not likely to be one with which a nation need reckon. To have reached a point in percentage strength equal to that of only fifty years after its founding is unlikely to engender strong consideration of the nation at large. There indeed may be 9 million United Methodists; but with nearly 250 million Americans, a shrinking percentage belonging to the denomination translates into a major loss of influence at the national level.

17

The Church School

In addition to church membership, the membership and attendance of United Methodists at the church school on Sunday morning demonstrates a remarkable decline over the past twenty years. In his seminal study of the period of 1949 to 1975, Warren J. Hartman clearly documented the decline in both church school membership and church school attendance.[4] In the 1960–64 quadrennium, church school enrollment reached the all time high of 7.8 million men, women, and children. By the 1980–84 quadrennium, the last complete set of quadrennial statistics, the enrollment had dropped to 4.1 million! This represents a phenomenal reduction of 47 percent of those enrolled in the church school. But should we believe that enrollment figures are devastating, church school attendance during the same period has plummeted by 50 percent from 4.2 million to 2.1 million individuals! Hartman demonstrates, in addition, over a six-year period from 1970 to 1975, the decline in church school enrollment by percentage of U.S. population. In the case of children age 0-11, a 23 percent reduction in enrollment occurred from 4.70 percent of the population to 3.62 percent. For youth aged 12-17, a 24 percent reduction in enrollment occurred with a decline from 4.71 percent of the population to 3.56 percent. For adults 18 years old and older, the reduction in enrollment was 16 percent, from 1.48 percent of the population to 1.24 percent.[5] He reports that for children this decline occurred at a rate three times as fast as the decline in the overall population of children in the United States. He also writes of the missing generation, those individuals in the 19-34 age group. It is this age group that is severely underrepresented in United Methodist congregations. Only about one-eighth of our members falls into this age bracket. But about one-fourth of the U.S. population is in this age group.

> This is our missing generation. They are a part of those commonly referred to as the baby boomer generation. Their absence from our churches, is without question, a major factor in our church membership decline.[6]

Somehow individuals in this age group were lost to The United Methodist Church before they reached the age of confirmation.

Even during the mid-fifties, while the U.S. birthrate was climbing, the number of infants being baptized in Methodist and Evangelical United Brethren churches was falling. By the late fifties a significant decline in the number of confessions of faith occurred. Most of the early baby boomers dropped out of the church sometime following baptism but prior to confirmation. By the time the baby boomers reached the age of confirmation the number of confessions of faith had fallen by one-half. Hartman states that since 90 percent of United Methodist net growth occurs through those individuals joining the church by confession of faith, the failure to "reach and hold onto the baby boomers who were born between 1946 and 1964 was a major causal factor in our church membership decline."[7] What went wrong with our church schools during this period?

In *Facts and Possibilities*, Douglas Johnson and Alan Waltz state, "The internal environment of The United Methodist Church from the late 1950s through the late 1970s was governed primarily by concerns related to the two issues of integration and merger."[8] This issue of denominational merger consumed an inordinate amount of denominational time and energy. Obviously it was perceived as an appropriate step toward the development of a stronger and larger United Methodist Church. However, the question may safely be raised in retrospect as to whether or not this step was the correct one for either denomination. Alan Walker of Australia once remarked to one of us (JWH) that the most devastating thing that had happened to him in his lifetime was to lose his church. This remark referred to the creation of the Uniting Church of Australia, composed of the former Methodist, Presbyterian, and Congregational Churches. Should Alan be correct in his own feelings, it may be that the 1968 union was an impetus for decline in both the number of congregations in The United Methodist Church as well as the number of members.

In 1987, Douglas W. Johnson, director of Research for the National Program Division of the General Board of Global ministries, published *A Study of Data from Former Evangelical United Brethren Churches, 1968–1985*. His study demonstrates that during the 1975–1985 period 28 percent of the total churches lost within The United Methodist Church in the United States were former EUB churches. This is clearly disproportionate to the proportion of EUB churches in the union (7 percent). He states:

"Most of The United Methodist Church closings occurred between 1968 and 1975, while the largest percentage of closings for former Evangelical United Brethern churches took place between 1975 and 1985."[9] Also of note is the fact that the former EUB churches had an average worship attendance decline of 25 percent, a rate nearly twice (13 percent) that of the denomination as a whole during the period studied. During the same period the former EUB churches noted a decrease of nearly 50 percent in average church school attendance while that of the entire denomination was only 37 percent. Johnson further points out that reductions in church attendance may have been exacerbated in former EUB churches by feelings of disinterest replacing a basic loyalty to the former denomination. He found that leaders in the former EUB Church believed that members of EUB churches involved in mergers "were not always positive toward losing their identity and facilities."[10] Consequently, the experience of The United Methodist Church with its merger with the Evangelical United Brethren Church is consistent with Alan Walker's personal experience and may have been mirrored by a similar experience of EUB members on a personal level. This observation causes us to question the wisdom of further unions within the framework of the Consultation on Church Union. Not only was the former EUB Church decimated by the effects of the union, but the new United Methodist Church expecting to be markedly strengthened by the union likewise failed to reap the expected benefits of the union.

Evangelism and Education

Undoubtedly there are many reasons why mainline Protestant denominations have lost members for so many years. Lyle Schaller, in *It's a Different World!* points out that during the eighty-year period from 1900 to 1980, the white population of the United States dropped from 85 percent to 78 percent.[11] He found that the various mainline Protestant denominations used two different strategies to reach the non-white population. One of these he called "inclusion," the other "evangelization." He found that the first strategy was used by Lutherans, Presbyterians, and Methodists. These denominations emphasized quotas to ensure that Blacks, Asians, Native Americans, Hispanics, and women obtained positions on regional and national denominational agencies. Doing so ensured that non-white individuals could influence the direction of policy and the use of denominational funds. In addition this approach encouraged the integration of ethnic minorities into existing congregations consisting primarily of white individuals. These denominations then embraced the melting-pot philosophy of inclusion of ethnic groups.

Schaller points out that while the Presbyterians and Lutherans were busy creating new denominations and the United Methodists made ethnic local churches the missional priority in fund-raising, the Assemblies of God and the Southern Baptist Convention used the second strategy: evangelization. Their goal was starting new congregations, not making sure that Blacks, women, and ethnic immigrants were fully represented in the denominational policy decision-making bodies. In the case of Hispanic congregations, by 1985, the Southern Baptist Convention included more than 2,000 Hispanic congregations, the Assemblies of God had more than 1,000, while the United Methodists had approximately 250. Schaller states that the Southern Baptist Convention is now the most inclusive Protestant denomination in the United States. By the end of 1985 it included 600,000 Black members who were members of nearly 1,000 congregations. For other ethnic groups the Southern Baptists had 466 Native American congregations involving 97 tribes, 151 Chinese congregations, 85 Laotian, and 77 Vietnamese. If the purpose or goal of our churches is to reach and serve people through local congregations, it is clear that the strategy followed by the Assemblies of God and Southern Baptist Convention has been more productive than that followed by the Presbyterians, Lutherans, and United Methodists. Perhaps our denomination has been more interested in responding to societal pressures than to reaching people for God. This information triggers several additional questions. First, what is our status in developing new congregations of any type? Second, what is the status of evangelism in our denomination at the national level? Third, in the light of the decline of Sunday schools,what is the state of education at the national level?

James Cowell, director of congregational development of the General Board of Discipleship, has stated that "the correlation between the number of congregations and the growth of a denomination is significant enough to say that no denomination will

21

be able to reverse its numerical decline without significant intentional effort in new church extension."[12] One of the most amazing aspects of merging the Central Jurisdiction and the Evangelical United Brethren Church with The Methodist Church during the 1960s and 1970s with the simultaneous structural overhaul has been the sapping of the evangelistic fervor of the denomination. This can most clearly be demonstrated by the major decline in new church starts across the denomination. During the 1950s and early 1960s the denomination was actively starting new churches. However, during the period from 1968 to 1983 the number of new churches started ranged from a low of 10 in 1971 to a high of 55 in 1982. Of 626 new churches begun during the period of 1966 to 1983, 93 were Asian, 18 were Hispanic, one was Black, and three were Native American.[13] During roughly the same period more than 20 million dollars were allocated to the Ethnic Minority Local Church missional priority.

Johnson and Waltz have reminded us that in 1963, the *General Minutes of The United Methodist Church* reported on a study of new churches that suggested a need for an additional 1,145 new churches by 1964! Needless to say, these congregations were never formed. In fact, in the middle 1960s church extension efforts disappeared. These authors fascinatingly demonstrate that during the period 1958–1961, while the U.S. population was growing by 9 million, The Methodist Church started 124 churches each year. From 1966 to 1984, while the U.S. population was growing by 36 million, the denomination started only 44 churches per year. Beginning with 1980, the number of new church starts has increased to more than 50 per year. "The highest percentage of new church starts has been before 1970 and after 1980."[14]

A denomination in a maintenance mode will not be starting new congregations. But if a church wants to double its membership in an eight-year period, it will of necessity have to be willing to organize new congregations. Part of our fascinating heritage as The United Methodist Church is the story of C. C. McCabe, assistant secretary of the Church Extension Society for the Methodist Episcopal Church. During the period from 1868 to 1884, he developed a major effort of church extension, resulting in the formation of congregations all across the United States. As he was traveling by train across the nation, McCabe read a newspaper account of Robert Ingersoll, the famous agnostic. Ingersoll had stated that "the churches are dying out all over the land; they are struck with death." McCabe left the train and sent a pithy telegram to Ingersoll that read:

Dear Robert: All hail the power of Jesus' name—We are building more than one Methodist Church for every day in the year, and propose to make it two a day![15]

If we as a denomination are serious about growing, let alone doubling our membership, we must be about the business of starting new congregations and building churches. At least one annual conference, Virginia, has developed a sense of urgency in the area of church growth and revitalization. Under the leadership of Bishop Robert M. Blackburn, this conference developed a campaign entitled "Revealing Christ: A Program of Congregational Growth." The 20 million dollars raised from this program will be used to plant new congregations and revitalize existing local churches. Of even more importance has been the fact that 75 percent of the money raised has been pledged by individual small contributors from the local congregations. More than 25,000 individuals or families have become involved. Startling success stories have been prevalent with many churches not only accepting goals greater than requested, but far exceeding even the accepted goal. The campaign itself at the local church level has become a major source of positive storytelling, as the local congregations have become imbued with the importance of the effort.

As we look at evangelism and education, the heartbeat of any denomination, we need to be aware of what the restructuring that began after the 1968 union of The United Methodist Church cost the denomination. As it is currently structured, the General Board of Discipleship has relegated these two key areas to section status in the Division of Nurture. As a result of this restructuring, as clearly stated by Warren Hartman,[16] funds distributed to these two key areas have steadily declined as a percent of the average annual contributions to general causes within the denomination. During the 1949–52 quadrennium, 5.08 percent of the funds for general causes were expended by education and evangelism. This level steadily declined to the 1973–76 quadrennium, at which time it reached 2.88 percent.

During the period from 1975 to 1986, using the third year of the quadrennium as an average year except for the 1985–1988 quadrennium when the most recent available data (1986) was used, funds allocated for evangelism and education decreased from 1.84 percent in 1975 to 1.16 percent in 1986 when compared to the total World Service Fund dollars available (Figure 3). Not only was there a steady erosion of funds allocated to these two key areas as a proportion of World Service Fund dollars, but within the General Board of Discipleship itself, the percent of funds allotted to evangelism fell from 26 percent in 1975 to 11 percent in 1986. In like fashion, funds allotted to education decreased from 21 percent in 1975 to 16 percent in 1986. Thus there has been a major change in priorities during the past forty years, which has resulted in a major decrease in funds allocated to the areas of evangelism and education. It is difficult to analyze the different studies because accounting practices have changed over this period and administrative overhead for the General Board of Discipleship has been assigned to the sections on Evangelism and Education. But the percentage of funds expended by education and evangelism has clearly become smaller.

The net result of this decrease in spending for evangelism and education may have in some major fashion contributed to the overall membership loss. With the creation of the General Board of Discipleship in 1972, the network of individuals active in education and evangelism at the general church and annual conference level was steadily eroded and has now disappeared. Not only have these precious resources been allowed to wither, but no longer do these two key areas vie for funds with the areas of Christian social concerns or missions. They now must vie internally within the General Board of Discipleship for funds with Worship, the Laity, and Stewardship.

In the area of evangelism, due to concern about a lack of evangelical focus, the General Board of Global Ministries has launched a Board-wide Committee on Mission Evangelism. The new committee will have several explicit functions, set forth by the Board. They are: (a) locate and identify places and groups of people without a Christian witness or where the witness has not been heeded; (b) in consultation/cooperation with mission partners, develop strategies for initiating these ministries within and among

FIGURE 3

Comparison of Expenditures for Evangelism and Christian Education 1975-1986

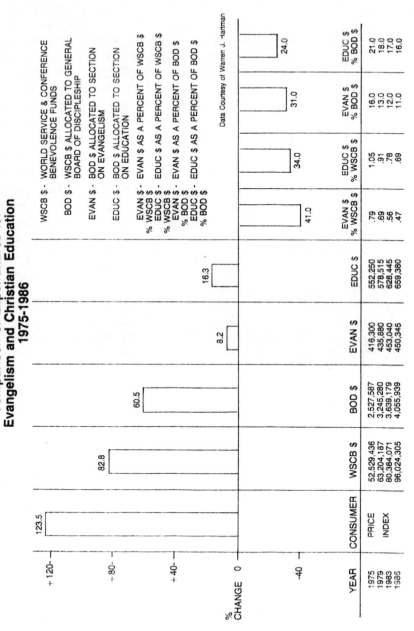

	CONSUMER PRICE INDEX	WSCB $	BOD $	EVAN $	EDUC $	EVAN $ % WSCB $	EDUC $ % WSCB $	EVAN $ % BOD $	EDUC $ % BOD $
% CHANGE	123.5	82.8	60.5	8.2	16.3	41.0	34.0	31.0	24.0
1975		52,529,436	2,527,587	416,300	552,250	.79	1.05	16.0	21.0
1979		63,204,187	3,245,280	435,880	578,515	.69	.91	13.0	18.0
1983		80,384,071	3,639,179	453,040	628,445	.56	.78	12.0	17.0
1986		96,024,305	4,055,939	450,345	659,380	.47	.69	11.0	16.0

WSCB $ - WORLD SERVICE & CONFERENCE BENEVOLENCE FUNDS

BOD $ - WSCB $ ALLOCATED TO GENERAL BOARD OF DISCIPLESHIP

EVAN $ - BOD $ ALLOCATED TO SECTION ON EVANGELISM

EDUC $ - BOD $ ALLOCATED TO SECTION ON EDUCATION

EVAN $ % WSCB $ - EVAN $ AS A PERCENT OF WSCB $

EDUC $ % WSCB $ - EDUC $ AS A PERCENT OF WSCB $

EVAN $ % BOD $ - EVAN $ AS A PERCENT OF BOD $

EDUC $ % BOD $ - EDUC $ AS A PERCENT OF BOD $

Data Courtesy of Warren J. Hartman

these places and groups, taking other interdenominational relationships into account; (c) working through appropriate units of the National and World Divisions, consult and coordinate with other boards and agencies of The United Methodist Church and ecumenical agencies; (d) nurturing newly gathered communities of Christians leading to the establishment of United Methodist or other congregations, enable them to be linked to The United Methodist Church through the missionary outreach of the General Board of Global Ministries; (e) consult with appropriate units with regard to the missionary selection, training, and placement processes of the Board with particular attention to the functions of mission evangelism; (f) expand support mechanisms for pioneer evangelism including prayer partnerships and support through Advance projects; and (g) for furthering the work of the board in interpreting the work of mission evangelism, engage in research and information gathering, model development, monitoring, and evaluation. Assist various units of the Board in interpreting the work of mission evangelism.[17]

With these objectives in mind, the General Board of Global Ministries will begin to lead the way forward in mission to the world. In order to place this ambitious effort in motion, the General Board of Global Ministries sent a petition to the 1988 General Conference calling for a program to be entitled "Mission 2000: The Key to Vital Congregations." This program directly supports the call of the Council of Bishops for an initiative entitled "Vital Congregations—Faithful Disciples." The delegates to the 1988 General Conference enthusiastically endorsed the proposal. However, at no time during the discussion on the floor of the General Conference was the question raised about the relationship of this program to the Section on Evangelism of the General Board of Discipleship. It would appear that the General Board of Discipleship may no longer be seen as the major proponent of evangelism within The United Methodist Church. An effort designed to develop vital congregations that are defined as organizations to produce faithful disciples[18] would appear to be clearly within the jurisdiction of the General Board of Discipleship. The location of such a program within the General Board of Global Ministries may be sending a clear message to the church that in the area of evangelism the General Board of Discipleship is no longer a key player. Surely a section of a division of a board would be unable to match the ability of a general board to provide funding and program development.

Confession of Faith

Warren J. Hartman clearly points out in *Membership Trends* as well as various issues of *Discipleship Trends* that individuals joining The United Methodist Church in the United States by confession of faith have declined from the peak quadrennium of 1957–60. He states:

> It should not come as a surprise to discover that trends in the number who are received by profession of faith are more closely correlated with trends in church membership than any of the other procedures for adding or removing names from the membership roll.[19]

During the last quadrennium for which complete data are available (1980–1984), only 210,068 individuals per year were added to church rolls by confession of faith. This represents a 50 percent decrease from the highest levels in the 1957–60 quadrennium.[20] In addition, Hartman points out that even though a large number of those who make a profession of faith come through the Sunday school, this route has been diminishing steadily with the loss of Sunday school members. In 1976, he stated: "Since 1972 nearly 62% of those who have been received by profession of faith were members of the church school."[21] He noted that in some conferences the number was as high as 80 percent. In his study he makes a remarkable point—nearly 40 percent of all United Methodist churches in 1974 received *no one* by profession of faith. An additional 10 percent received only one person on profession of faith. This phenomenon is not due to small churches failing to have individuals who could be led to confessing their faith, since small churches actually received a larger number of individuals by profession of faith per thousand members than the larger churches. In his study, 222 churches with a membership of over 500 received two or fewer individuals in 1974 by profession of faith. It is astounding that nearly one-half of all United Methodist churches still receive no one by profession of faith. In fact, approximately one-half of all United Methodist churches do not even conduct a confirmation class each year.

27

Conclusions

Perhaps it should come as no surprise to us that as a denomination we have continued to decline in membership for the past forty years. Particularly during the past twenty years since the incorporation of the Central Jurisdiction and the union with the Evangelical United Brethren Church we have been caught up in structural changes, societal upheavals, and global concerns to the exclusion of processes of evangelism. We have markedly reduced our expenditures at the national level in the key areas of evangelism and education, while simultaneously watching our church and Sunday school memberships decline rapidly. We have sent a message, whether intentional or not, that these two vital areas are not nearly as important to our denomination as some other areas that seem to receive quite a lot of attention: global missions, the social issue agenda of Church and Society, the racial concerns of the General Commission on Religion and Race, the societal issues of the General Commission on the Status and Role of Women, and so on. We have failed to actively seek out the youth of our denomination and bring them into the church, either directly or through confirmation classes.

As a result, we have watched our influence wane as a national force in the United States. We now constitute a church that reaches the same proportion of the American population as it did 150 years ago! Had we simply kept pace with the highest level that we reached soon after World War II, our denomination would now have over 15 million members. The issue is clear. The United Methodist Church must reverse its decline and once more resume its place as a major actor on the stage of the American national scene!

CHAPTER 2

A Kept Clergy?

And I heard the voice of the Lord saying, "Whom shall I send, and who will go for us?" Then I said, "Here am I! Send me!" And he said, "Go, and say to this people . . ." (Isa. 6:8-9).

While in the Temple mourning the death of his good friend King Uzziah, Isaiah has a vision in which he sees God as holy, and whose glory is reflected throughout the whole earth. In the presence of a Holy God, Isaiah knows he is unclean and that he lives in the midst of unclean people. He cries out to God! After experiencing God's forgiveness and cleansing, Isaiah hears God calling, "Whom shall I send, and who will go for us?" Isaiah's response is, "Here am I! Send me!" God calls Isaiah to be a prophet, *a spokesperson for God,* to Judah, a nation that has turned away from justice, righteousness, and true religion. Through Isaiah, God speaks to this nation telling her that she is on a collision course, but *there is an alternative,* God's way!

In the twentieth century, just as in Isaiah's day, God continues to seek out men and women and ask, "Whom shall I send, who will go for us?" "Who will be my spokesperson for this generation?" Many have heard and responded by saying, "Here am I! Send me!" However, there is a haunting question that Isaiah's experience keeps asking, Am I answering God's call on my life? Or, am I answering the call of a profession? Or, have I interpreted God's call correctly?

* * * *

Ministry in The United Methodist Church may be divided into two groups of individuals. The ministry of the church specifically acknowledges the priesthood of all believers. As United Methodists we believe that every Christian is a minister of the Lord Jesus Christ within the context of his or her specific vocation. In The United Methodist Church this is the foundation of all true and authentic

29

ministry. Dennis M. Campbell of Duke Divinity School has stated: "Baptism, the sacrament by which persons are initiated into the Christian community, may be thought of as an admission to the general ministry of the church."[1] Although all Christians are called to ministry in the church of Jesus Christ, throughout the history of Christianity some individuals have been called to a ministry that has set them apart. This is what is known as the representative ministry, which results from the act of ordination.

Specifically since the New Testament period, the church has set apart some individuals to provide leadership for the community of faith. "These leaders were to articulate the gospel of Jesus Christ, to teach the faith, to help others practice the faith in daily life, and to be exemplars of the faith representing Christ to the church and world."[2] Scripture speaks to the roles of deacon, elder, and bishop, but these terms are not precisely developed. However, over time as transmitted to the United Methodists of today, these three roles became a part of the itinerant ministry of our denomination. Wilson and Harper[3] state: "John Wesley made use of ordained persons whenever possible, especially in the administration of the sacraments, preaching the gospel, and the general oversight of the United Societies." Although ordained himself as a priest of the Church of England, Wesley heavily utilized lay preachers in his movement. In Great Britain, this was not a major difficulty since there were many opportunities for individuals involved in the Methodist Societies to participate in the sacraments through the Church of England. However, during the early days of American colonization, particularly on the frontier, there was a major shortage of ordained individuals, resulting in difficulty in providing the sacraments. Lay preachers, the circuit riders of the early frontier, were not authorized to administer the sacraments, thus creating a significant hardship. As a result, Wesley ordained men to serve in America.

The story of Wesley's decision to ordain Methodist clergy for America and later for Scotland, Newfoundland, Nova Scotia, the West Indies, and for England itself, is a fascinating one. Soon after Methodist lay men and women began to arrive in the American colonies, Methodist lay preachers began their work. But since Wesley refused to allow the lay preachers to administer the sacraments, significant pressure began to build for ordained clergy to provide for this function. This became particularly acute following the American Revolution, since there were virtually no Anglican clergy present in the new nation. By 1784, there were 14,998 Methodists in the newly independent United States who were served by 83 lay preachers. Wesley asked the bishop of London to ordain some of his lay preachers; but when the bishop refused, Wesley, who saw himself as a scriptural bishop, decided to ordain the preachers himself. Wesley had long since come to the conclusion that he was a bishop in the New Testament scriptural sense, being the superintendent of the Methodist portion of the Church of England. He particularly believed that it was a responsible act to ordain individuals to serve in the United States because there was no national church such as the Church of England. He therefore ordained two preachers as deacons on September 1, 1784, and the following day ordained them as elders to serve in America. Thomas Coke, who was already an elder in the Church of England, was ordained as a superintendent and was sent to America to serve with Francis Asbury in the leadership of the new church. Coke was directed to ordain Asbury and the two of them were to ordain other preachers. As he so often did, Wesley acted in a pragmatic way to assure the success of the new church in America. The result of Wesley's action was the development of the ordained clergy of one of the predecessor denominations of The United Methodist Church.

Professionalism

For years the ordained person has been viewed as a member of a profession, a profession not unlike medicine, the law, and others. At the same time, individuals who have heard the call of God upon their lives have been ordained and have become a part of the clergy. Therefore as a profession the ordained ministry is significantly different from other professions. As called individuals, ordained ministers are expected to perform the role of servant, not only in regard to their congregation, but as servants to the world. Historically, this has usually meant salaries significantly lower than those in other professions. "[T]he role of the pastor-teacher with his or her parishioners is different, because [they] are not called to practice theology as a profession. No, [they] are called to live the faith."[4] Thus the basic nature of the ordained ministry differs from that of other professions.

R. Sheldon Duecker (now Bishop Duecker), in his book *Tensions in the Connection*, written as a part of the Into Our Third Century series, has cogently stated the difficulties that have arisen within the clergy due to the perception of professionalism. The first of these is the issue of salary. There is a rapidly growing belief that the financial disparity between the clergy and other professions should be abolished. That there is a significant disparity between the ordained ministry and other professions in the realm of remuneration is clear. But Bishop Duecker also reminds us that there is a difference between providing an adequate living and being paid at a level commensurate with the other professions. At the same time some laypeople, who are unwilling to compensate their pastor adequately, complain of their pastor's inability to understand the economic system of the United States. But many United Methodist pastors have been excluded from the economic system of the United States by virtue of being paid disproportionately to their ability, education, and effort.

Second, Bishop Duecker writes of the result of professionalization, which may cause members of the clergy to view their activities as a career, rather than a calling. Thus ordained ministers who are planning their careers are not necessarily following the "call to preach." "A professional ministry derives its authority from the organization, while a called ministry receives its authority from God."[5]

Third, Bishop Duecker states that professionalization of the clergy results in professionals separating themselves from non-professionals. In this he explicitly cites the development of a language that only other professionals can understand. He also notes that a key element of professional status is involved with the protection of the prerogatives of the profession. Such activity within the church could result in an increasing clerical domination of The United Methodist Church.

Although we believe most United Methodists today would applaud their clergy's becoming more professional, a word of caution is necessary. Generally speaking, a person who is recognized as a professional commands a certain degree of status and power within the community—and, we must admit, sometimes seems to relate best to other professionals. But for many United Methodists who live in small congregations far removed from the suburbs of America, a pastor to whom they can relate in an intimate fashion is far more important than any other factor. If professionalism creates a wall of separation between the pastor and the flock, then indeed it becomes an offending eye or hand!

An Itinerant Ministry

In *Rekindling the Flame*, William H. Willimon and Robert L. Wilson set the tone for the issue of the itinerant ministry by entitling their chapter that covers it—"Serve the Church Instead of the Clergy!" From the beginning of American Methodism, clergy have been sent, not called. By so doing our denomination has developed an ordained ministry in which pastors are not members of the local church they serve, but members of the annual conference in which they have been ordained. As itinerant, or traveling ministers, they are under appointment by the bishop serving their area. They are therefore "sent" by the bishop to the church they will serve. Consequently, United Methodist ministers are not "called" by the local church they serve. As a result each local church is provided a minister and each minister is provided a church to serve. "To operate effectively, the system requires that each pastoral charge must receive and support the appointed minister, and that each minister must serve faithfully the church to which he/she is appointed."[6]

In the appointment-making process, the bishop, under the rules of *The Book of Discipline*, has the final authority to make the appointment of the pastor to each local church. However, during the past several decades, a rising tide of wanting to be a part of the appointment process has swept over the United Methodist laity. This desire has been realized to some extent with changes to *The Book of Discipline* in which the local church Committee on Pastor-Parish Relations has been brought into the decision-making process. This process is known as consultation and is defined in *The Book of Discipline* as "the process whereby the bishop and/or district superintendent confer with the pastor and Committee on Pastor-Parish Relations . . . . Consultation is not merely notification. Consultation is not committee selection or call of a pastor. The role of the Committee on Pastor-Parish Relations is advisory. Consultation is both a continuing process and a more intense involvement during the period of change in appointment."[7] However, as Bishop Duecker states, "While *The Book of Discipline* makes clear that authority for pastoral appointments rests with the bishop, the practice of consultation causes local church leaders to believe they do the actual hiring and firing."[8] This confusion needs to be addressed in the near future if The United Methodist Church is to continue to have an effective appointment process and to have a "sent" clergy. *The Book of Discipline* also states that United Methodist clergy "offer themselves without reserve to be appointed and to serve, after consultation, as the appointive authority may determine."[9] Consequently, the bishop, district superintendent, pastor, and local church are all involved with the appointment through the process of consultation, but the bishop, as the appointing authority, makes the final decision, which results in the pastor itinerating.

A crucial aspect of the appointive system of our denomination is the seniority of the minister. Usually, ministers advance through their careers by moving to another local church that pays a slightly higher salary than that of their previous church. The new church also is usually somewhat larger than the previous one. Such a system has the appearance of rewarding faithful service irrespective of competence or the possession of the requisite gifts and graces of servant ministry. Appointments made as a reward have made it increasingly more difficult for the denomination's churches to maintain their vigor, as demonstrated by the loss of members across all five jurisdictions. As a consequence the usual avenues of career progression are becoming more limited, and this limitation will continue to result in marked difficulties in the future. Johnson and Waltz have pointed out that "the perception is widely held by both ministers and laypersons that the appointment process increasingly is being used to solve the organizational problems of the conference as a whole and is not focused on serving the best interests of either the individual minister or the local church."[10]

In the seniority system, a system that is informal but nonetheless real, pastors are expected to move through a continuum of service. Some first serve as associate ministers or as pastors of multi-church charges. Some serve single churches from the very beginning. As experience is gained they move to larger and larger churches whose salaries are usually higher than that of the previous local church. There is some significant rigidity in this system, because it is unusual for appointments to be made out of sequence. One of us (JWH) is aware of two local churches in which major difficulties have existed for years. Both churches have essentially been pastored by individuals who were moving steadily through the seniority system. Both churches were in the process of dying. One was an old-line large, now inner-city church, which historically was one of the highest salary churches in its conference. As a result older senior pastors were assigned to the church and it continued its steep decline. In order to attract younger people who would have to pass several United Methodist churches to reach this downtown church, a vigorous, effective younger minister was needed, not one who was appointed because it was his due. The second church in another conference had declined by fits and starts as it served the needs of the conference for a location for the appointment of pastors who had other significant conference responsibilities. As a result of serving the needs of the conference first, the needs of the local congregation were not always successfully met. In this latter instance, the bishop appointed a pastor in his late thirties with a record of turning around declining churches. The result has been a complete turnaround in the history of this local congregation.

In addition to seniority in length of service and participation in all appropriate conference activities, salary plays an important role in the appointive system. Willimon and Wilson have said that "the myth prevails that the higher the salary, the more effective the pastor."[11] All local churches are urged to keep the salaries as high as possible, with the presumption that a high salary will result in an effective pastor. Laypeople often believe that a correlation exists between a high salary and a quality pastor. In a system of supply and demand such might well be the case. However, in The United Methodist Church the seniority system will produce a pastor who has served the conference well and who is due a local church with a higher salary. In the case of the local church first mentioned above, an effective pastor who could attract people to an urban church was assigned only after the laypeople of the congregation had taken the drastic step of lowering the salary in order to reset their location in the seniority system of the conference. In the case of the second church, the salary had been allowed to erode dramatically during a period of high inflation. Simultaneously the church had been in financial straits that had effectively resulted in an inability to keep the salary at its previous level in terms of real dollars. Both churches were able to have younger ministers appointed simply because the low salary resulted in a younger minister. Johnson and Waltz make the point succinctly: "The emphasis should be on providing leadership for the ministry needs of the congregation, not solely the personal, financial, or professional needs of the minister. Commitment and competence must be placed high on the list of criteria for apppointment."[12]

In addition to seniority and salary as determinants of ministerial appointment, involvement in conference activities may be important. Certainly in some conferences this is less a part of the appointment process than in others. Pastors who spend large amounts of time outside their local church in peripheral activities, which may be good and important in themselves, but which are not important to the local congregation, may find themselves in trouble in their ministry. This trouble may occur simply because they do not spend their time doing the hard work of servant ministry—preaching effectively, teaching dynamically, and calling consistently. These efforts may not be glamorous, but they are intensely longed for by the laypeople of the local congregation.

Laypeople want effective spiritual leadership regardless of the size or prestige of the local church. They want pastors who are readily available when they are needed. "Today, people are confused and lonely, overstimulated and bewildered. They want a familiar friend, a pastor they know, and a spiritual leader who can take them spiritually deeper than they have ever gone before."[13] They really do not care if their pastor is a volunteer chaplain, president of the grade school PTA, involved with United Nations trips with a group of conference youth, or even president of the district ministers' organization. They want their pastor effectively at work in their local church *first*. If the preaching, teaching, and calling meet the needs of the laypeople, then the laypeople are more likely to accept and encourage avenues of personal and professional growth for the pastor.

Ministerial Competence

One of the most difficult issues facing our denomination is that of ministerial competence. Every conference has a small number of clergy members who move virtually every year, never rising above the level of minimum salary. Every bishop and cabinet must know that these incompetent and ineffective pastors will have a devastating impact on a significant number of congregations during their careers. It is true that bishops must appoint all individuals in full connection with an annual conference after they have already been approved by district and conference Committees on Ordained Ministry, so responsibility for ministerial competence does not rest entirely at the top. It is also true, however, that a person's actual level of competence sometimes might not become clear until well after the requirements for a guaranteed appointment have been fulfilled.

Stories abound in every conference about these individuals. One such story is told of a United Methodist minister who was noted for being late nearly every week for the eleven o'clock worship service. A visitor to his home one weekend overheard the following conversation after the minister's daughter knocked on her father's study door:

"Come on, Daddy, we'll be late for church!"

"I'll be there in a minute, honey, I still need one more point for my sermon."

Somehow as a denomination, we must come to grips with this issue of competence.

Competency or lack thereof is not a chargeable offense, or at least it should not be. The call of an individual to the ordained ministry is between that person and God. But God does not call people to be United Methodist ministers. That determination is made by mechanisms that have been established by the church. It is on this basis, for example, that The United Methodist Church has made the decision not to ordain self-avowed, practicing homosexual individuals. At the same time that we set standards of conduct for those entering the ministry as well as standards for them to maintain during their ministry, we have failed to establish useful mechanisms for dealing with incompetent ordained ministers. Standards of competence and mechanisms for gracefully allowing incompetent pastors the opportunity to leave the United Methodist ministry must be developed, along with a valid system of appraisal. The time has come when protection of the incompetent members of the annual conference can no longer be allowed.

The system of guaranteed appointments has a major impact on the protection of incompetent ministers. The guarantee of an appointment is found in *The Book of Discipline*, which states: "All clergy members who are in good standing in an Annual Conference shall receive annually appointment by the bishop unless they are granted a sabbatical leave, a disability leave, or are on leave of absence or retired."[14] The guaranteed appointment provision of *The Discipline* requires the bishop to appoint all ministerial members of the annual conference, in essence, irrespective of competence. Evaluation of ministers is now the responsibility of the Committee on Pastor-Parish Relations of the local church, the district superintendent, and the bishop. For example, *The Discipline* states: "There are professional responsibilities which clergy members are expected to fulfill and which represent a fundamental part of their accountability and a primary basis of their guaranteed appointment."[15] But the same paragraph also requires that pastoral effectiveness be evaluated annually by the Committee on Pastor-Parish Relations and the district superintendent, who are to be trained in the processes of evaluation so they can determine the gifts, health, and readiness for ministry of the ordained minister. In addition, the paragraph states that growth through continuing education is expected.

The Discipline provides two major methods for dealing with incompetent ministers. They may either voluntarily or involuntarily be placed on leave of absence status or their membership may be terminated (Pars. 448 and 453.3). In the case of an unrequested leave of absence, the minister involved has the right to a hearing before the bishop, cabinet, and executive committee of the Board of Ordained Ministry. In the case of administrative location, the minister has right to a trial. It is obvious from the pertinent portions of *The Discipline* that competency is basically viewed as an issue of discipline, not evaluation and/or appraisal. A major effort needs to be made to provide for useful evaluation or appraisal of the ordained members of the annual conference. Using this evaluation, appropriate steps need to be established for individuals to be relieved of their duties as United Methodist ministers in an administrative methodology, not a disciplinary system. Incompetence is not the equivalent to moral turpitude!

In some instances, no matter how hard Boards of Ordained Ministry work to prevent it, some less than fully competent individuals will become United Methodist ministers. To treat them as we would individuals who fail to maintain the high standards of our denomination from a moral perspective is unfair. Just as some individuals do not reach the standards for ordination in The United Methodist Church, others may fail to reach or maintain the standards of competence. Our denomination must have a methodology for dealing with these individuals in a humane manner.

But the issue of guaranteed appointments goes farther than simply the issue of competence. Guaranteed appointments make necessary a system to deal with incompetency since such appointments protect all individuals, including those who are incompetent or of borderline competence. Lazy pastors are also protected by this system. With the declining number of local churches within The United Methodist Church, the number of pastoral appointments is also falling. It is possible to visualize a situation in which an annual conference would be unable to ordain new clergy members into the conference because there are already enough pastors available to fill all the appointments. In such a case highly competent new seminary graduates would not be ordained and become members of the conference while less than fully competent individuals would continue to serve the churches of the conference. This may not be a problem in that a number of United Methodist ministers will retire in the coming years and certainly some conferences are concerned with finding enough pastors to fill all the appointments. Nevertheless our churches deserve to have appointed to them the best ministers that we can provide.

Evangelism and Teaching

Bishop Richard B. Wilke has aptly pointed out that "if leadership praises and rewards pastors for evangelism and education in the parish, vibrant growth will occur."[16] He indicts many United Methodist pastors by displaying the statistics for 1985. In the 1985 annual reports of the local churches in the United States, 16,093 (42 percent) reported no constituency roll or prospect list! Sixty percent or 22,912 churches reported no membership training or confirmation classes! In 1985 14,423 churches (38 percent) received no one by confession of faith and over 67 percent (25,662 churches) received four individuals or less! Of all our churches 31 percent (12,026) did not baptize a single person—no one—in 1985! Is it unfair to ask what our United Methodist ministers are doing? Have our efforts dropped because of our inadequate emphases on evangelism and education? Bishop Duecker answers these questions by stating that "changes in motivation suggest that the historic United Methodist sense of evangelism is being replaced. Instead of evangelical witness, the denominational concern seems to be moving in the direction of trying to solve the world's problems through the church."[17] Perhaps our denomination could use these statistics to evaluate the effectiveness of our pastors.

The basic tools of ordained United Methodist ministers obviously must include the ability to win people to Jesus Christ and to equip people for the general ministry of the church through preaching and teaching. As detailed in chapter 1, Warren Hartman has demonstrated that our denomination has failed to grow, in fact has lost members, due to our failure to win people for Christ through church membership. The route of confession of faith for membership in the church has fallen dramatically over the past twenty years. We must assume that we are not equipping our ministers for the work of evangelism either at the seminary level or through continuing education. In addition we are not holding them accountable either for winning new people for Christ or for equipping them as general ministers of the church. The Reverend J. O. Craig has been a United Methodist minister for more than sixty years. During that time he has held himself accountable to the Lord he serves for the new members of the church. Although he had a very successful career in active ministry, including serving large churches and providing leadership at the conference level as a district superintendent, his personal record of the growth of his churches was based not on the number of individuals who joined by transfer of their membership, but on the number of those who joined by confession of faith. Even while serving a small rural church as a supply pastor, following his retirement at age seventy-two, he continued to count the increase of his flock by numbering the new conversions. His conference did not hold him accountable in this manner, but as a person called to servant ministry, he held himself accountable to the Lord he loved for his ministry. Somehow, The United Methodist Church has failed to maintain a sufficient level of accountability for its pastors.

Recently, the new *Disciple* Bible Study has become available for use in United Methodist congregations. There appears to be a resurgence of interest on the part of ordained ministers for the teaching function of their ordination, perhaps simply because it is now expected that they will participate in this new effort to provide some scriptural literacy for United Methodist laypeople. Or perhaps the time has come for them to take seriously the teaching function of their ordination. Our pastors are ordained as deacons prior to being ordained as elders. As such they have been ordained to a teaching function, since the deacon has the authority to preach the Word as well as to perform other duties (conduct worship, witness marriages in the states that so permit, and conduct funerals). Then, as elders, these individuals have "full authority for the ministry of Word, Sacrament, and Order."[18] Willimon and Wilson state that "in the Wesleyan tradition the pastor is always the chief Christian educator in the congregation."[19] At some point we have apparently lost this significant function as a major role of our pastors.

Our pastors are not the only ones who have failed the laypeople of our denomination. The General Conference in its wisdom restructured the general agencies of the United Methodist Church and by so doing both education and evangelism have lost the visibility and vitality they once enjoyed. Can we blame our pastors if they have accurately determined the prevailing attitudes within the denomination? Clearly neither education nor evangelism has been considered *really* important during the past twenty years. *Disciple* is the first serious effort at Bible study in our denomination in years. In addition, only recently have several of our United Methodist seminaries established chairs of evangelism and begun once again to seriously teach evangelism to their students. Until annual conferences are willing to require individuals preparing for ordination to have training in evangelism, it is doubtful that we will effectively equip our pastors for this major role.

Conclusions

In order to field an effective clergy, The United Methodist Church must develop a system of accountability that is fair, effective, and sufficient. Incompetent ministers must be allowed to leave the ministry of The United Methodist Church in a compassionate fashion. Incompetence is not moral turpitude. But some individuals who are ordained, for whatever reasons, may not be capable of a long-term ministry within our denomination. A methodology must be created to allow them to leave gracefully. Our local churches deserve a trained, effective clergy. We must remember that evaluation "is not only a means for making better appointments, but also a way of developing more skillful pastors through accountability."[20]

Our ministers must regain the ability to effectively lead our congregations in winning people to Christ and to equip laypeople for the general ministry of the church. Until our ordained ministers are willing to be the chief educators of the local church and are willing to count the *real* increase in the Body of Christ, The United Methodist Church will continue to decline in members and influence within our nation.

Bishops and cabinets must seriously consider the needs of the local churches as they work within the United Methodist system of itineracy. The needs of the churches must be paramount. We have ordained individuals into the servant ministry of Jesus Christ. By so doing we have taken individuals who have been called by God and set them apart for service. We must not allow itineracy to become "like a union which rewards the members not necessarily because of ability, but because of persistence and longevity."[21] We need ministers whose appointments are based on the needs of the local churches. A clergy so deployed will be far more effective than one deployed based on considerations of seniority, salary, or conference requirements.

CHAPTER 3

Is the General Church Irrelevant?

Therefore, brethren, pick out from among you seven men of good repute, full of the Spirit and of wisdom, whom we may appoint to this duty (Acts 6:3).

Have you ever wondered how and why the first agency of the church came into being? The answer to this question is found in Acts 6:1-6. The young church in Jerusalem was experiencing growth in numbers, even priests were coming into the Christian faith, but an internal problem developed over the distribution of food to widows. The Greeks felt the Hebrew widows were being favored in the daily distribution of food. There was much discussion and discontent over this matter.

The twelve disciples called a meeting of the church to discuss the problem. Believing that God had called them to preaching and prayer, the disciples did not want to add the distribution of food to widows to their responsibilities. The community of faith (church) decided to form an agency to carry out this task. Seven men, whose lives are described as full of the Spirit and wisdom, were chosen for the task. This greatly pleased the church and, after prayer and the laying on of hands, the seven men began carrying out this special ministry.

It is not surprising that the purpose of the first church agency was to assist the local church in carrying out its ministry, for today, even with the multiplicity of agencies of The United Methodist Church, the purpose of each remains the same as in the first century. The general agencies exist to assist the local church in its mission and ministry to the local congregation and community.

* * * *

The general church structures of The United Methodist Church are those agencies that function on a national or international level, acting for the entire denomination. Bishop Earl G. Hunt, Jr., in his book *A Bishop Speaks His Mind*, analyzed them as follows:

The United Methodist Church undertakes to conduct its far-flung mission under the guidance of four major *program* boards, two of which (the General Board of Global Ministries and the General Board of Discipleship) are actually *mega-boards*, and two *focus* boards (the General Board of Higher Education and Ministry and the General Board of Church and Society); two *advocacy* commissions (Religion and Race and Status and Role of Women); three *service* commissions (Archives and History, Communications, and Christian Unity and Interreligious Concerns); two *support* boards (Pensions and Publication); two *administrative councils* (the General Council on Ministries and the General Council on Finance and Administration); and two *constitutional* councils (the Council of Bishops and the Judicial Council).[1]

Bishop Hunt continues by saying that due to the nature, size, and scope of their activities, an enormous amount of power is concentrated in these agencies of The United Methodist Church. In fact, much of the general church structure is of significant importance to the local church and its members. If such is the case, why are these agencies perceived to be irrelevant to the local churches and the laypeople who sit in the pews?

The General Conference

The General Conference is established by the Constitution of The United Methodist Church to be composed of at least six hundred and not more than one thousand delegates evenly divided between lay and clergy, elected by the annual conferences. Article IV states: "The General Conference shall have full legislative power over all matters distinctly connectional," and "to enact such other legislation as may be necessary, subject to the limitations and restrictions of the Constitution of the Church."[2] In addition *The Book of Discipline* clearly states (Par. 610) that "no person, no paper, no organization, has the authority to speak officially for The United Methodist Church, this right having been reserved exclusively to the General Conference under the Constitution."[3]

In contrast to the general church agencies, the General Conference has a marked effect on the laypeople of the local church. As the denomination-wide governing body, its legislative activities express the polity of the denomination. The decisions made by the General Conference delegates directly affect virtually all United Methodists. It is the only way that changes can be made to *The Book of Discipline*. In addition to forming and passing legislation, the General Conference also perfects and approves resolutions that speak to the church largely on the social issues of the day. It is in the resolutions that most United Methodists are affected. Some issues that are handled legislatively have a significant impact on the laypeople of the local churches; but many of these items are technical, dealing with ministerial pension programs and other aspects of any major corporate entity.

The General Conference lasts less than two weeks and is held every four years. Although large amounts of material are sent in advance to the delegates by both the Commission on the General Conference (*Advance Daily Christian Advocate*) and the various general agencies of the church as well as the several caucuses, there is little time for the delegates to absorb all that is sent. More than 2,600 petitions were submitted to the 1988 General Conference held in St. Louis. Each petition was acted on by one of twelve legislative committees. In turn each was brought before the General Conference as a committee of the whole. Many were dealt with by use of the consent calendar. This system, devised some years ago by Judge Jerry Bray of the Virginia Conference, and now Rule 27 of the General Conference, allows petitions unanimously approved by a legislative committee to come before the General Conference and be passed without debate.

The major difficulty for General Conference delegates is time. There is simply not enough time for each delegate to review adequately each major issue or individual petition and to be knowledgeable about them. However, one of the most remarkable aspects of the General Conference is that each United Methodist, lay or clergy, may petition the General Conference. Two individuals from Virginia worked diligently to make an impact on the General Conference on two issues of importance to them. One individual believed strongly that the word "catholic" in the Apostles' Creed should be defined in a footnote in the new hymnal. The other strongly believed that each local church should have a United Methodist Men's unit as *The Discipline* requires for United Methodist Women. He had worked on this issue at every General Conference since 1968! At the 1988 General Conference both petitions were approved. These stories are not isolated examples. Each petition is read and is debated, at least in the legislative committees, and each petition can be debated on the floor of the General Conference as long as at least one delegate requests that it be done.

Due to time constraints, however, during the last several days of the General Conference the rules of debate are usually changed. This is done in two ways—by limiting the number of speeches that can be made on either side of an issue and by limiting the length of each speech. Late in the General Conference, speeches are usually limited to one speech on each side of an issue and may be limited to one minute. Since many of the most controversial resolutions are placed on the agenda during the waning days of the General Conference, a full debate is rarely possible. At the same time items may be placed on the consent calendar that had ten or even twenty votes in opposition in the legislative committee. It is at this point that the system breaks down. In order for the General Conference to act on every petition, during the last day or two of the General Conference debate is quickly halted by the new rules and more and more items that had significant opposition in the legislative committees are placed on the consent calendar. As a result many resolutions are passed without being properly debated by the General Conference. These are often the most controversial issues, which are most likely to produce the greatest negative reaction by the laypeople in the local churches.

Since the actions of the legislative committees are of such importance, it is worthwhile to consider how their membership is derived. In all annual conferences, membership on the legislative committees is determined by the order in which the delegates are elected by the annual conference. Once that order is determined, each delegate, in the order elected, selects the legislative committee he or she prefers. Each delegation is allowed to place only one member on each committee until all legislative committees have a member from that conference's delegation. Through the years it has become obvious that members of the boards of directors of the various general agencies as well as the staff personnel of these agencies prefer, if possible, to serve on the legislative committees that deal with the issues of their agency. Bishop Sheldon Duecker states that in these instances it is not unusual for such a delegate and general agency member to become an interpreter and advocate for legislation proposed by the general agency.[4] He continues:

Due to the delegate selection process and the weight given to agency positions, all petitions do not receive equal attention. Persons supporting and interpreting legislation in which they have a personal interest or investment exert a substantial influence in General Conference *even when the specific piece of legislation involved has not been reviewed from the perspective of the mission of the total denomination.* In this respect General Conference includes both special interest groups and people who have a special stake in the continued existence of the denomination's bureaucracy.[5]

Thus the presence of paid staff members of the general agencies of the church has a marked influence on the actions of the legislative committees. These staff members act not only as delegates and members of the legislative committees, but also as interpreters and lobbyists for the legislation their board or agency has proposed or supported.

In an effort to change this clear appearance of a conflict of interest, the 1988 General Conference voted:

Paid employees, whether executive, support staff or otherwise, of any general board or agency of The United Methodist Church shall be ineligible to serve as a voting member of a General Conference Legislative Committee which will act upon the programmatic or financial proposals of the general board or agency to which they are related.[6]

Although passed overwhelmingly with a 72 to 28 percent margin, the Judicial Council at its October 1988 meeting found the legislation to be unconstitutional. This effort by the 1988 General Conference was a clear indication of the feeling that the staff of the general agencies wield too much power within the structure of The United Methodist Church.

Besides serving on legislative committees that deal with issues of direct concern to their employment, staff members of the general agencies also exert significant, if not undue, influence on the General Conference by their presence in large numbers at the Conference. "The presence of general agency staff at General Conference also influences decision making. They often serve as resource persons for legislative committees and as advisors for the delegates. These persons *are not staff of the General Conference* but of the agencies which are proposing legislation and seeking financial support for the next quadrennium."[7] The seriousness with which this large presence of general agency staff is viewed was specifically addressed by the 1988 General Conference. The 1984 General Conference requested that the amount paid for expenses of general agency staff be reported to the 1988 General Conference. In the *Advance Edition of the Daily Christian Advocate*[8] the General Council on Finance and Administration reported that 203 general agency staff members were present at the 1984 General Conference at a cost of $247,517 ($1,219 each). The number of individuals present by general agency ranged from a high for the General Board of Global Ministries with 59 staff members present to a low of two individuals present from The United Methodist Publishing House (not including book and resource display staff). The 1984 General Conference requested that the general agencies provide in advance the names of those staff members who would be attending the 1988 General Conference. A total of 225 staff members were expected to attend the 1988 General Conference, of whom 46 served on the staff of the General Conference or its treasurer, or served as working press, press staff or video crew.[9] Of the 225 general agency staff members present in 1988, 63 were staff members of the General Board of Global Ministries.

At the 1988 General Conference, the General Council on Finance and Administration recommended that the general agencies confirm their staff members present at the Conference and provide a report of their expenses to the 1992 General Conference. In addition is was recommended that: "Representatives of the general agencies meet with the General Council on Finance and Administration to establish the criteria and number of agency resource persons needed for the 1992 General Conference."[10] During the floor debate this recommendation was amended to require that no general agency exceed the number of 40 staff members at General Conference.[11] The amendment passed with a 60 percent affirmative vote. During the discussion it was confirmed by Bishop Joseph H. Yeakel that the per diem limitations established for delegates to the General Conference did not apply to the staff of the general agencies.

This action to limit the number of staff members present at the General Conference may well have been a reaction to the perception that general agency staff members were heavily lobbying the delegates for certain legislative actions in which they were interested. Delegates could observe that many of the speeches made on the floor of the General Conference had either been previously written (many were typed) or were brought onto the floor of the General Conference by pages. With staff members costing at least $250,000, it was clearly perceived by a majority of the delegates that a smaller number could adequately perform the staff duties required at the Conference.

In 1983, Bishop Duecker in *Tensions in the Connection* stated: "Undue influence of the general agencies at General Conference may well have contributed to hostility found among pastors and local churches toward general agencies and their programs. Thus, tension and frustration have been generated by the issues of appropriate role and balance of influence at General Conference."[12] Bishop Duecker's statement may well reflect the position of a majority of the delegates at the 1988 General Conference. The perception, regardless of the facts, was that there was a far greater presence of general agency staff than was required to conduct the business of the Conference. Douglas Johnson and Alan Waltz, both senior staff members of general agencies, have stated that "the interests of the local church have a difficult time being represented [at the General Conference] unless they correspond, or at least do not conflict in some significant way, with the agendas of the general agencies."[13] The members and staff of the general agencies recognize that if their legislation and resolutions are passed in the legislative committees there is an extremely high probability that they will be passed by the General Conference. The two pieces of legislation detailed above from the 1988 General Conference were clearly efforts to reduce the power of the staff of the general agencies to impact on the actions of future General Conferences.

General Agencies

Most United Methodist laypeople have little or no contact with the general agencies of our denomination. As a consequence these national church agencies have little or no relevance to the life of the local church. This statement is perhaps an oversimplification, but to a large extent it is an accurate perception of the situation. There may be a number of reasons for this perception, not least of which is the size of the four program boards, particularly the General Board of Discipleship and the General Board of Global Ministries. The size of these mega-boards has tended to make them impersonal bureaucracies. Some laypeople perceive the general agencies to be indifferent to their needs and particularly indifferent to their concerns. Bishop Duecker has stated the position succinctly:

> There is widespread distrust of the agencies by pastors and laity alike. Agencies are considered to be far removed from the local congregation, unwilling to respond to correspondence, addressing themselves to clientele other than the local church, creating problems because of controversial stands on social issues, and conducting unnecessary and overlapping functions. For many United Methodists, the general agencies represent "the other church."[14]

The members of the general boards and commissions are selected in several ways. In the United States, first, an annual conference nominating committee composed of the bishop and the General and Jurisdictional Conference delegates selects individuals who will be a part of a jurisdictional pool of candidates from which the Jurisdictional Nominating Committee selects individuals for election. The 1988 General Conference provided that all General Conference delegates in the United States would automatically become a part of the jurisdictional pool. In addition, each annual conference is authorized to nominate at least fifteen additional individuals (and not more than forty) in eight specific categories: clergy (including at least one woman), laywomen, laymen, racial and ethnic persons, youth, young adults, older adults, and persons with a handicapping condition.[15] This action of the 1988 General Conference should have a rather dramatic impact on the number of individuals in the nominating pool of each jurisdiction. In addition it will result in giving key leaders in each annual conference an opportunity to be considered for general agency membership.

Various formulas provide for the membership of each general agency. In the case of the four program boards, each annual and missionary conference in the United States and Puerto Rico is allowed one member. The names of all individuals nominated by the annual and missionary conferences but not elected by the jurisdiction are placed in a pool from which additional members may be elected. The 1988 General Conference amended *The Discipline* such that "it is recommended that at least 30 percent of a jurisdiction's membership on each general program board be racial and ethnic persons."[16] And additional individuals elected by the general agencies to provide for inclusiveness and special knowledge or background that would aid in the work of the agency are not required to be elected from the remaining names in the jurisdictional pools.

As the past practices of the denomination are reviewed in this area, Johnson and Waltz state that "the membership of the program boards and the General Council on Ministries comes to these agencies now because they represent some group—an Annual Conference, youth, clergy, laymen, laywomen, racial or ethnic minority, and handicapping condition. For most of the boards the additional membership is generally used to complete the required representation in various categories rather than to bring into the membership persons with 'special knowledge or background.' "[17] Due to the manner in which individuals are elected to the general agencies, as well as the requirement that no one serve more than eight years on a particular agency (except on the General Board of Publication), it is quite difficult for board members to have the required knowledge and skills. It is therefore difficult for the members to have the experience and knowledge needed to make the appropriate informed decisions. "The lack of knowledge also tends to place additional power in the hands of staff."[18]

The staff members of the general agencies have become the center of much of the controversy surrounding the general structure of The United Methodist Church. Since there is no chief executive for the church, the general agencies seem to function in an autonomous fashion. As a consequence there is a growing disillusionment with the apparent lack of accountability. This concern has been expressed by efforts to set tenure limits on the elected members of the staff. The 1984 General Conference established a twelve-year-tenure rule for ordained ministers serving under appointment in these positions. Since a uniform tenure rule was not established for lay and clergy alike, the Judicial Council ruled the legislation invalid. However, the 1988 General Conference reestablished the twelve-year-tenure rule for both lay and clergy elected staff members to take effect January 1, 1989. This legislation allows for extensions beyond twelve years by a two-thirds vote of the board members. This effort has been clearly directed at a perceived indifference by the staff of some of the agencies to be responsive to the laypeople of the denomination.

Bishop Earl G. Hunt, Jr., has made certain observations concerning the staff of the general agencies. He generously commends the necessity of bureaucracy within our church, since it is clear that due to its size and complexity this form of organization is virtually mandatory. However, he states that the bureaucracy must carefully consider the concerns of the laypeople of the denomination, particularly "when significant issues are being decided and important pronouncements crafted."[19] There is a clear perception on the part of some grassroots laypersons that the pronouncements (which General Conference has approved) of the general agencies are often out of step with their beliefs and are inimical to their best interests either as Christians or citizens. This may simply be due to honest disagreements over the social issues of the day, among others, but some stances of general agencies are embarrassing to some church members. Many perceive that the effort has been made to dress political issues up as religious and moral issues in an effort to somehow obtain God's blessing on them. Since most of these church pronouncements are viewed to be closely aligned with the liberal political agenda, many local church members with different political persuasions are alienated from the general church structures. We believe that the staff of the general agencies play a major role in these endeavors.

Bishop Hunt makes several points that deal with the issue of such pronouncements of the general agencies. First he states that "the agencies must remember always that they never speak *for* the church, but only *to* it."[20] He also adds that the church members must remember that the agencies are impelled to speak prophetically to the church. However, some laypeople have difficulty with many of the prophetic utterances because they appear to have a one-sided thrust to them. Roy Howard Beck, a religion reporter, in his memoirs entitled *On Thin Ice* (Bristol Books, 1988), speaks directly to this issue as he provides background material for many of the stories he reported during his tenure as a reporter for *The United Methodist Reporter*. His book deals with a perceived bias of the denomination's bureaucracy and the concern of laypeople with this issue.

Second, Bishop Hunt states that "the great boards must never move too far ahead of where the people are, and they must be willing to listen sincerely to input from intelligent conservatives as well as liberals among their members and throughout the church."[21] The bureaucracy of the church must realize they cannot lead if they are out of sight of those being led. In such a situation the leader simply becomes irrelevant. We believe that this is the current situation in The United Methodist Church.

Bishop Hunt further states: "All of our agencies, of course, must administer faithfully the actions of the General Conference, even when those actions are not pleasing to them. It perplexes the church and destroys the credibility of boards and agencies when directors or staffs, albeit subtly, work in behalf of positions contrary to those taken by General Conference."[22] Two general agencies during the 1988 General Conference were sent a powerful message over their perceived indifference to the desires both of the General Conference and the church at large. By a surprising vote of 482 to 460, the General Conference narrowly defeated a minority report that would have terminated the General Commission on the Status and Role of Women. A switch of only twelve votes would have resulted in this agency's being abolished.[23] This action was certainly surprising in that virtually no agency of the church is ever abolished! As Wilson and Harper cogently state: "A great deal of time and energy goes into attempting to ensure that the General Conference will continue the various agencies and provide the needed funds."[24]

In another surprising move, nearly 60 percent of the delegates at the 1988 General Conference voted to conduct a study on the feasibility of moving the General Board of Global Ministries from its current location on Riverside Drive in New York City.[25] This effort, which would partly be an economic move and one that would make the General Board of Global Ministries more accessible, was also partly directed at the staff of the board because of the feeling that "the agenda for the local church is set by the church bureaucrats who have a particular interest and area of responsibility."[26] Some laypeople across the denomination are concerned that the General Board of Global Ministries, particularly the staff, seems unresponsive to the needs and concerns of the local church. This lack of concern has been demonstrated in numerous ways which can be most readily summarized as a we-don't-care-what-you-think attitude. This perceived attitude may have played a role in the General Conference action to study the feasibility of moving it.

Bishop Duecker has set forth a reasonable rationale for the actions of the general agencies staff members:

> Bureaucratic structures allow opportunities for general agency staff to meet regularly for interaction, planning, evaluation, and implementation. This is a proper and necessary set of functions. As a result of such opportunities, these groups gain much more influence and cohesion than those staffed by volunteers, whose endeavors are not nurtured by regular and extended association. In short, the staff of agencies are full time, while bishops and elected members give only part-time attention to programming.[27]

Due to such power, the staff of general agencies have a major responsibility to the membership of the church to maintain a balance as well as credibility in their actions. Failure to do so, or a perceived failure to do so, may result in efforts by the General Conference to require accountability for their actions. Some of the actions of the 1988 General Conference were directed precisely at the issue of accountability. Should the staff of the agencies fail to recognize their responsibility for clear accountability to the church at large, additional efforts requiring it to do so will occur at future General Conferences.

Caucuses

Although not a part of the official structure of the church, the various caucuses, nevertheless, perform many of the same functions. Over the past twenty years a variety of these organizations have been created. Several such organizations have racial and ethnic origins. They were developed to deal with the concerns and injustices within the denomination. The four major racial or ethnic caucuses are: Black Methodists for Church Renewal, Methodists Associated Representing the Cause of Hispanic Americans (MARCHA), Native American International Caucus, and the Asian American Federation. These organizations have their own staff, meet regularly, and seek support for those issues that are important to them. In addition they receive funding from the World Service apportionment through the Minority

Group Self-Determination Fund, which expended nearly one million dollars each year in the 1985–88 quadrennium.[28] Thus all United Methodists share to some extent in their advocacy activities. These caucuses raise additional funds through a variety of efforts. Of the most interest is the quasi-official status of this particular group of organizations, although none of them are official general agencies of the church.

There are other caucus groups within the denomination. One of the most significant is Good News, the Forum for Scriptural Christianity. Others include Affirmation, the caucus of gay and lesbian concerns. One of the oldest such organizations is the Methodist Federation for Social Action, which tends to support activity in the arena of social policy. As Wilson and Harper demonstrate, "They usually highlight issues or groups that they feel the denomination is either ignoring or minimizing. They monitor the denomination when they perceive segments of it to be violating official policy in theology or polity. As such, the caucuses play a prophetic role in the denomination."[29] The caucuses play a basically positive role in the denomination, holding it accountable for a variety of issues the church needs to address.

Unfortunately, however, the creation of the caucus movement within the church has had a tendency to polarize the leadership of the church. Leaders for the ethnic and special issue caucuses have emerged, but their leadership has been developed to lead specific groups involved with particular issues. "Leaders of these caucuses had no intention of being leaders for the denomination."[30] They have specifically been interested in making the church responsive to their particular agenda. Within their particular organization they have become functional leaders. Their leadership has continued because they have been able to form an organization with which they have a community of interest. Therefore, in some respects, the caucuses have deprived the entire denomination of major leadership.

Quotas

It is impossible to write of general agencies of The United Methodist Church and not include the quota system which currently exists. As indicated earlier, it is recommended that at least 30 percent of the membership on each general agency board be racial or ethnic persons. As a church that is less than 5 percent racial or ethnic in membership, The United Methodist Church has recommended a strong imbalance in favor of racial or ethnic groups. This effort to provide an opportunity to ethnic individuals to be a part of the decision making of the denomination has, in turn, disenfranchised the majority. The quota system was devised at a time when the denomination was uniting with its own Central Jurisdiction and with the Evangelical United Brethren. At this time a major effort was perceived to be needed to bring all individuals in the denomination into the mainstream of its leadership. However, as time goes by, it is becoming more obvious that the quota system has outlived its usefulness. Indeed it may be that the quota system perpetuates an underclass within the church as the majority sees that minority individuals must be protected. Election of individuals should be based on ability alone. The quota system "can have a long-term impact on the role the agencies fulfill if they are perceived to be primarily the preserve of special-interest and ethnic groups and not identified with the broad range of United Methodist people."[31]

Conclusion

Willimon and Wilson and Hunt have clearly pointed out that much of the work of the general agencies is worthwhile. But it appears that the perceived interests of the general agencies may not be the interests of the local church or its lay membership. The three authors point out that one of the major negative effects of the organization of the general agencies is to communicate to the members of the local church that the really important actions of the denomination occur out in the general church arena and not in the local church or the community in which it resides. They also indicate that the activities of the local church may be set by the general agencies, thus relieving the local church congregation of the responsibility for being the church in their own community.[32]

Over ten years ago, Jameson Jones, then president of Iliff School of Theology in Denver, Colorado, stated that the test of the general agencies of the church was *"whether or not they facilitate vital ministry, whether or not they help the church fulfill its mission."*[33]

The general agencies are to inform, educate, and resource local churches (via annual conference structures) to the approved (by General Conference) policies, priorities, and goals of The United Methodist Church. Indeed, the general agencies of The United Methodist Church are irrelevant unless they undergird and support the local congregation as it finds itself in mission to its community and to the world.

CHAPTER 4

What Theology?

That you [individual and communal] may be filled with all the fulness of God (Eph. 3:19*b*).

In Nathaniel Hawthorne's writings, there is a delightful story called "The Great Stone Face." The central character is a lad named Ernest who lives in a little village in the valley. High on the mountain over the village is an outcropping of rocks which form the face of a noble, pleasant, kind man. This magnificent work of nature is called the Great Stone Face. Ernest spends hours looking at this face, even talking to it at times. Ernest developed a close bond with the face.

An old legend circulating in the valley says that at some future day a child will be born who is destined to become the greatest and noblest personage of his time, and whose countenance, in manhood, should bear resemblance to the great stone face. Ernest yearns to see this person in his lifetime but, just as in previous years, the prophecy has not been fulfilled. Ernest grows old and his hopes begin to fade. But, one evening as Ernest is in the village talking with his many friends, a poet in the midst shouts, "Behold! Behold! Ernest is himself the likeness of the Great Stone Face!"[1] Ernest, through the years of looking at and admiring the Great Stone Face, and believing the prophecy, had come to embody those very characteristics that he loved and found present in the face. This story illustrates why it is so important to know and discuss Wesleyan theology. We become like what we hold dear, what we meditate on, what we yearn for.

* * * *

Theology comes from two Greek words: *Theos*, meaning God, and *logos*, meaning word or rational thought. Theology, then, is a word or rational thought about God. The purpose of theological study is summarized in the scripture that introduces the chapter,

59

"That you [individuals and communal] may be filled with all the fulness of God." The theological task is never finished, it becomes a continuing process for "every generation must appropriate creatively the wisdom of the past and seek God in their midst in order to think afresh about God, revelation, sin, redemption, worship, the Church, freedom, justice, moral responsibility, and other significant theological concerns."[2] Or, to say it another way, the study of theology is an ongoing process of learning how to love God with all the heart, soul, and mind. And, learning to love neighbors as self.

United Methodists Hold Dear

Before discussing what United Methodists believe, it is necessary to define the meaning of the word "believe." Often words become so familiar that we seldom ask the meaning. It is also possible for the English meaning to be quite different from the original. This has happened to the word "believe," for its current English meaning is "the holding of ideas." This has not always been its meaning, for literally and originally "believe" means "to hold dear."[3] Therefore, when United Methodists say, "I believe . . . ," they are not just holding ideas; what they are saying involves more. To believe is an investment of the total person: heart, mind, soul, and body.

The following are doctrines United Methodists "hold dear." They are not exclusively Wesleyan doctrines, for United Methodists have no affirmations that are not also believed by other Christian groups. What is unique is the way they are believed. In writing about United Methodist beliefs, we are well aware that words, no matter how carefully chosen, cannot adequately express the full meaning, for beliefs are always beyond language. However, in the study of theology, it becomes necessary to try.

United Methodists Believe in God

The three most important letters in the English alphabet are GOD, for what we believe about God determines how we relate to ourselves, to others, and to the world. United Methodists believe in *one God* who is infinite in wisdom, power, and love. We believe that *God as creator* brought forth a universe of order, purpose, and meaning. As a part of creation, God made men and women in the divine image so that fellowship and partnership could be experienced between God and individuals (the covenant community).

Humanity was given a special feature, different from all other living creatures—human freedom. Humans are not automatons; they are set free with the ability to mold life. Using this gift of freedom, sin, an inner condition of rebellion against the Creator, entered the human family. God could have said, "I am through with the human race." However, being a *God of grace*, God graciously took the initiative on humanity's behalf to offer to all people redemption and reconciliation. United Methodists believe God's grace, which is God's extravagant goodness toward us, is experienced in three dimensions: "God's grace goes before us (prevenience), God's grace comes among us uniquely in the person of Jesus Christ (justification), and God's grace abides with us restoring our lives to an unrelenting love for God and neighbor (sanctification)."[4]

Another way of explaining God's grace is this: God is *for* us! God loves us as if each of us is an only child. Being loved like this means:

being accepted without restrictions
being loved regardless of whether we return it or not
being offered the vast resources of God
being forgiven and restored to full relationship
with God when we repent
experiencing everlasting love

Bishop Emerson Colaw tells about a former governor of Wyoming, Milward Simpson, and his wife who were in an airplane that developed trouble. When the pilot announced he was going to try an emergency landing, the governor took the hand of his wife and they offered this statement of faith:

The light of God surrounds us,
The love of God enfolds us,
The power of God protects us,
And the presence of God watches over us;
Wherever we are, God is.[5]

Living or dying, we are in God's care. This is what is meant by God is *for* us. As George Morris states, "The realization that we are supported, surrounded, and sought by a final reality which we call 'love' is the most amazing, incomprehensible and marvelous fact of human existence."[6]

United Methodists Believe in Jesus

The New Testament tells the story of the greatest fact of history, the coming of Jesus the Christ (Messiah) into the world. Coming to earth in the form of humanity, experiencing life, and dealing with the same issues all humankind faces, Jesus, through example and words, taught us to experience and respond to life in such a way that the kingdom of God will come on earth as it is in heaven. This involves loving one's neighbor, extending and accepting forgiveness, serving wherever there is human need, praying for those who despitefully use you. In so doing individuals experience abundant living both now and in the age to come.

We believe that Jesus "is the image of the invisible God" (Col. 1:15), and in him "all the fulness of God was pleased to dwell, and through him to reconcile to himself all things" (Col. 1:19-20). The resurrection was God's stamp of approval that Jesus was truly God's son in whom God was well pleased. Through the life, death, and resurrection of Jesus, humanity can experience salvation (wholeness). We believe that Jesus not only proclaimed the kingdom of God, but was the kingdom of God breaking into history.

Christian was the name given the followers of Jesus. His call, "Follow me!" continues to go forth to *all* people. Answering in the affirmative means to be yoked with Christ and a co-worker with him in bringing reconciliation, redemption, and renewal to a world God loves and seeks to be in *shalom*.

United Methodists Believe in the Holy Spirit

United Methodists know God as creator, God as revealed in Jesus Christ, and God as Holy Spirit within us now for guidance, comfort, and strength. In the section entitled "Distinctive Emphases of United Methodists" in the Doctrinal Statements of the 1984 *Book of Discipline*, there is this sentence: "One of the most familiar accents in traditional United Methodist teaching has been on the primacy of grace. By grace we mean God's loving action in human existence through the ever-present agency of the Holy Spirit."[7]

Wesley emphasized vitally experienced religion occurring through the power of the Holy Spirit. On a recent visit to City Road Chapel in London, one of us (EL) was deeply moved by the repeated use of the encircled dove around the gallery. The guide stated that Wesley chose this symbol to be a reminder to persons of the eternal presence and power of the Holy Spirit who encircles our lives. According to Bishop Mack Stokes, Wesley taught on the basis of scripture "that the Holy Spirit is present and active in *every major stage of Christian experience.*"[8] In the first stage, Wesley believed that the activity of the Holy Spirit as *prevenient grace* goes forth to all persons while yet sinners, encouraging and calling persons to open their lives to the transforming power of God.

In the second stage of Christian experience—repentance, forgiveness, experiencing the new birth (conversion)—*justifying grace* through the Holy Spirit is present. According to Wesley, this new birth is the beginning of inner righteousness (right relatedness with God, self, and others). Paul speaks of this experience in these words: "Therefore, if any one is in Christ, he is a new creation; the old has passed away, behold, the new has come" (II Cor. 5:17). This re-creation cannot be done in one's own power, neither can it be earned through good works or purchased with money; it is through the grace of God at work in the Holy Spirit. In this new life, the witness of the Spirit comes to announce that such persons are *sons* and *daughters* of God (Rom. 8:15-16; Gal. 4:6-7).

E. Stanley Jones states there are three fruits of conversion that result when individuals become sons and daughters of God. Persons pass from estrangement from God to become children of God. The second fruit is "the change of relationship to yourself. You have been forgiven by God and now you can . . . forgive yourself. All self-hate, self-despising, self-rejection drop away and you accept yourself in God, respect yourself, and love yourself." The third fruit "is an altered relationship to others." You cease to move away *from* people, and you cease to move against people. Instead, you begin to move *toward* people in love. "God moved toward you in gracious love and you move toward others in that same outgoing love."[9] In such interrelatedness, Christian perfection becomes a continuing process.

This moves us to the third stage of Christian experience, the growth or maturing process. Wesley writes, "A child is born of a woman in a moment, or at least in a very short time: Afterward he gradually and slowly grows, till he attains to the stature of a man. In like manner, a child is born of God in a short time, if not in a moment. But it is by slow degrees that he afterward grows up to the measure of the full stature of Christ."[10] Just as the nature of a newborn baby is to grow, so it is with us in the spiritual life. We are instructed by Jesus to "be perfect, as your heavenly Father is perfect" (Matt. 5:48). What a challenge! Reaction to this command is generally, "That is not possible." From a human standpoint it is impossible, but the Holy Spirit, as *sanctifying* grace becomes the power in shaping lives toward that goal. It is both a human process and a divine reality. Wesley calls this process Christian perfection.

For Wesley, Christian perfection does not mean that individuals become finished or complete as one could say of a work of art or a piece of music, but rather, to be perfect in love, that is, in intention and attitude. Today the pure love of God is invited to flow into the heart, mind, soul, and body. Tomorrow the same. This process is described in Ephesians 4:15, "Speaking the truth in love, we are to grow up in every way into him who is the head, into Christ." Wesley believed that Christian perfection, or holiness of heart and life, is the goal of God for all creation; and God not only desires it, God is actively involved in producing it.

No section on the Holy Spirit would be complete without mentioning the oft-spoken phrase, "a Spirit-filled person." For Wesley, a Spirit-filled person is one who embodies the Spirit of Jesus. The life of Mother Teresa is a living example of a Spirit-filled individual. As a nun who headed a girls' boarding school in Calcutta, India, Mother Teresa felt within her a call of God beyond this position. As she was riding through the streets of Calcutta on her way to a retreat, she became "overwhelmed by the sight of abandoned persons, lying in the streets, left to die. Some of these forgotten people were already having their not yet lifeless limbs gnawed by rodents. Under the impact of these grim sights she felt a call to a new form of vocation—a ministry of presence, service and care to the abandoned, the forgotten, the hopeless."[11] A

Spirit-filled person is one who is a co-worker with Christ in a ministry of love wherever there is human need.

United Methodists Believe in the Holy Bible

The position of Scripture in Wesleyan theology is well established in the writings of Wesley himself. In a letter to John Newton, April 24, 1765, Wesley writes, "In 1730 I began to be *homo unius libri*, to study (comparatively) no book but the Bible."[12] In his preface to his first collection of *Sermons on Several Occasions* (1746), he proclaims his intention to be *homo unius libri*, a man of just one book. That "one book" was the Scripture and one cannot read the works of Wesley without becoming aware that he was rooted and grounded in Scripture. As Dr. Albert Outler states: "Wesley *lived* in the Scriptures and his mind ranged over the Bible's length and breadth and depth like a radar tuned into the pertinent data on every point he cared to make."[13] Wesley did not mean in *homo unius libri* that other books were excluded from his reading list for he recorded after 1725 most of his reading, and this record shows more than fourteen hundred different authors, with nearly three thousand separate items from them.[14] What Wesley did mean was that the Bible was his first and final norm for the validation of any theological discussion. In Wesley's words, his religion was "the religion of the Bible."

In matters of doctrine, Wesley was committed to the principles of religious toleration and doctrinal pluralism, but was confident of a "marrow" of Christian truth that can be identified and that must be conserved. Therefore, full inquiry must take place within the boundaries defined by four main sources and guidelines: Scripture, tradition, experience, and reason. These provide a broad and stable context for theology. However, while Scripture is only one of the guidelines, "United Methodists share with other Christians the conviction that Scripture is the primary source and criterion for Christian doctrine."[15] Scripture holds this unique position because United Methodists believe: first, the Bible is the record of the activity of God in human history. "It is the picture of human encounter with the action of the presence, purpose, and power of God in the midst of human situations."[16] Second, through the Bible God speaks to the brokenness of humanity and offers, as a gift, the way to salvation (wholeness). Third, even though the Bible is an ancient source of the memories, images, and hopes by which the Christian community came into existence, it is as up-to-date as the evening news. The issues of life remain the same: broken relationships with God, self, others; humanity's need for love; God's initiatives on behalf of individuals; God's alternative future for the world. Fourth, as hearts and minds are opened "to the Word of God through the words of persons inspired by the Holy Spirit, faith is born and nourished, our understanding is deepened, and the possibilities for transforming the world become apparent to us."[17]

In *Shaped by the Word*, John Mulholland has an interesting chapter on the "Iconographic Nature of Scripture." In it, he talks about Scripture as an icon; a window into the reality of God, Jesus, Holy Spirit, sin, redemption, broken covenants. As such Mulholland suggests the great need for persons to come to Scripture, stand before it, be open and allow the Scripture to speak and shape life. In such an approach, the Scripture addresses us. We are *shaped by the Word, not shapers of the Word.*[18] This formational approach to Bible study is quite a contrast to the informational style where gathering facts, dates, names, and places is the major focus.

Such an approach to Bible study was one of the hallmarks of John Wesley. He daily sought through study, questions, discussion, and prayer to be shaped by the Word. To illustrate, Wesley had been taught and sincerely believed that souls were saved by the two sacraments—baptism and the Eucharist—supplemented by works of mercy and help. Wesley believed there was no such thing as an instantaneous conversion. Being challenged on this belief by his Moravian friend, Peter Böhler, Wesley searched his Greek New Testament and discovered to his surprise that in the early church such sudden changes of heart were the rule rather than the exception. It was not long until Wesley's sermons focused on "For by grace you have been saved through faith" (Eph. 2:8a). The man Wesley had been shaped by the Word. As sons and daughters of Wesley, we must stand with open mind and heart before the Scripture so that we, too, may be shaped by the Word.

United Methodists Believe in the Kingdom of God

The central theme of the teachings of Jesus was the kingdom of God. In the parables, we see that this Kingdom is the prized treasure, the precious pearl. We are commanded to "seek first his kingdom and his righteousness." United Methodists believe that the kingdom of God is the divine rule of God in human society *now*, as well as in the age to *come*. As Perrin states: "The Kingdom of God is the power of God expressed in deeds; it is that which God does wherein it becomes evident that he is king . . . . It is quite concretely the activity of God as King."[19] As such, the Kingdom is already here; it is yet to come. It is a present reality; it is a future hope. Jesus spoke of the Kingdom as being within us, around us, among us, and beyond us. Jesus points to his own person, his work and ministry as the activity of the Kingdom. The miracles, the casting out of demons, healings, and forgiveness of sins are evidence of the Kingdom's arrival.

All of us are invited to enter the kingdom of God by a radical faith response to the sovereign God. The term *radical* is used because such invitations or proclamations as—"Follow me," "Seek first his kingdom and his righteousness," "You must be born again," "Go sell what you have and give to the poor"—demand a basic fundamental change of life. It involves total trust in and loyalty to the King of the kingdom. What results from this relationship is the kingdom of God experienced as *lived reality*. Or, as E. Stanley Jones said, "You become the Kingdom of God in miniature."

Jesus tells us that to enter the kingdom of God one must "turn and become like children" (Matt. 18:3). One can just imagine what was going through the minds of the group who heard Jesus make this statement. "Did Jesus say become as little children?" "Are you certain he said 'children'?" This would have been a shocking statement to everyone present because of the position of children in a country ruled by Roman law. Children were powerless, not powerful. Children were supposed to learn from adults, not adults from children. What a reversal of thought and life-style is being called for by Jesus! When Jesus said "turn," he uses a word that means a decisive turning, stopping in your tracks, turning and heading for a new destination. Jesus is saying, "Stop going in the direction you are now headed. Turn, go in the direction of becoming childlike."

What does it mean to become childlike? One of the first things that comes to mind is the depth of trust that a child places in those significant persons in his or her life. When one of our children (EL) was three years old, he would stand on the edge of the swimming pool and call out, "Catch me!" Without a moment of hesitation, he would jump into outstretched arms. Over and over he would repeat this action, confident that he would be caught. Could becoming childlike mean having that level of trust in God who waits with outstretched arms?

A second characteristic of children to which Jesus may be referring is their eager spirit. Children are very inquisitive and enthusiastic about the challenge of life. There is a natural openness to new ideas and new opportunities. Have you ever seen a closed-minded child? What a contrast is found between the eager spirit of a child and the stagnant spirit of a Pharisee! Could becoming childlike mean having a spirit of openness to God, to life?

A third characteristic of children is their ability to love deeply and respond to love. One of us (EL) has an eighty-six-year-old friend who, twenty years ago, decided that his "call" to ministry was to go each Sunday to the church school class for three-year-olds and tell them, "God loves you and I love you." John has taken this call very seriously and continues to do it every Sunday morning. Parents in that church will tell you that there were times when they came to Sunday school because of the persistence of their child. The children knew that John would miss them, and they also needed to hear John's special word of love. Could becoming childlike mean sharing with God and persons, as well as responding to love?

Another wonderful characteristic of children is their ability to relate to people regardless of social position, age, sex, or race. They do not form relationships by such criteria, but by the possibility of a fun playmate. A friend recently retired, and the day following his retirement he heard a knock on the door of his home. Mr. Whitaker's wife answered and found on the doorstep the three-year-old neighbor who asked, "Can Mr. Whitaker come out and play with me?" Needless to say, he could and he did. In the life of Jesus, we see that so often the issue with which he is dealing is division in the human family; Jews/Gentiles, rich/poor, male/female. Could becoming childlike mean that we do not use divisions to determine our relationships? That we see people as possible friends?

In summary, United Methodists believe that the kingdom of God is the activity of God in human society now and in the age to come.

Those who experience the Kingdom as *lived reality* are in a continual process of becoming like little children, becoming real. Is not this the meaning of the prayer, "Thy kingdom come, thy will be done, on earth as it is in heaven"?

United Methodists Believe in the Church

As children we used to sing in Sunday school, "I am the church, you are the church, and we are the church together." How true this is because the church is not a building with a tall steeple, but a community, a fellowship of true believers under the Lordship of Christ. The foundation on which the church is built is revealed in a statement made by Peter in response to Christ's question,

> "But who do you say that I am?" Simon Peter replied, "You are the Christ, the son of the living God." Jesus answered, "On this rock I will build my church, and the powers of death shall not prevail against it" (Matt. 16:15-18).

The rock is the identity of Christ, the son of the living God. Any church built on the rock will withstand political systems, persecutions, and denial of freedom to worship. Nations have tried to destroy the church, only to find through such actions, the church has been strengthened. Hitler, for example, "said the church was hollow and he could destroy it in a year, but the church has been an anvil on which a good many hammers have worn out."[20]

The local church is the strategic base for hearing the Word of God, worship, receiving the Sacraments, and where the spiritual nature of people can be nurtured. It is where individuals can encounter the living God. Putting into words the role and function of the church is difficult because these are always above and beyond language. That is why the New Testament uses metaphors. Perhaps the church is best described as the "Body of Christ." Using this metaphor as a guide, the church will be a community of love where we enter into a covenant relationship with God, with one another, and with the world.

Flowing naturally out of being a community of love is being a community of service. Servanthood becomes a way of life. The local church is the servant of the community. In the parable of the Last

Judgment (Matt. 25:31-46), we see that persons who had fed the hungry, clothed the naked, visited the sick, given water to the thirsty, welcomed the stranger, and visited the prisoner were invited to, "Come, O blessed of my Father, inherit the kingdom prepared for you from the foundation of the world." Being the "Body of Christ" involves being a community of love and a community of service. Or, serving in Christ's place!

In addition to the local church, The United Methodist Church "is also an inherent part of the Church Universal, which is composed of all who accept Jesus Christ as Lord and Savior, and which in the Apostles' Creed we declare to be the holy catholic Church."[21] In this vast connectional system, we have *nurturing* and *evangelistic* responsibilities to the global community, and the *structure* through which these can be extended. Truly, the world *is* our parish! Henry H. Tweedy of Yale University prayed for this great church:

O Spirit of the living God,
Thou light and fire divine:
Descend upon thy Church once more
And make it truly thine!
Fill it with love and joy and power,
With righteousness and peace,
Till Christ shall dwell in human hearts,
And sin and sorrow cease.

Conclusion

We have been examining Wesleyan theology—not rigid doctrines, but a way of being in Christian faith. Is this a theology that will awaken the giant? To answer, let us look to eighteenth-century England, the century of John Wesley. The social conditions of England closely parallel those of twentieth-century America:

The age was essentially materialistic
Many in the Church of England believed that God
was defeated and that Christianity was in its last days
For the most part the pulpit shrank from attitudes of positive leadership
The poor were nauseating to the aristocracy
Every sixth shop in London sold gin and drunkenness was the commonest of vices.

In this environment Wesley preached the theology we have been discussing, and it was the medicine for a sick century for "Wesley would build the Kingdom of God through the changed lives of individuals, whose collective holiness should work out the salvation of society. His medicine would go to the seat of the infection, and destroy its very germ!"[22] Literally thousands heard the good news that God loves all people and, even though all have sinned and come short of the glory of God, salvation is offered to all through God's grace by faith.

The great revival (awakening) began and spread across England. This revival changed the course of English history as Bishop William R. Cannon stated at the 1988 Southeastern Jurisdictional Conference, "John Wesley saved England from the bloody revolution that France experienced." Believing that America can be transformed by Wesleyan theology is not a foolish dream or an impossible goal. It is already a fact of history! And history can repeat itself!

CHAPTER 5

Does the Local Church Have a Role in Our Mission?

"Take heed to yourselves and to all the flock, in which the Holy Spirit has made you overseers, to care for the church of God which he obtained with the blood of his own Son" (Acts 20:28).

Paul is on board ship going toward Jerusalem. When the ship docks at Miletus, Paul sends for the elders of the church at Ephesus to meet him in order that he can talk to them. During the visit Paul reveals to the elders that he will not be with them again, and he wants the life and ministry of the church of Ephesus to be carried forward in a bold way. The power for such a task will come from the Holy Spirit. However, the elders must be willing for the Spirit to work through them.

This conversation lifts up how important the local church was to Paul. Ten books in the New Testament are Paul's letters to local churches, and First and Second Corinthians are two of these letters. When a local church that Paul had established was having problems and he could not return to it immediately, he wrote God's message to the people. We are privileged to have these letters in our Bible, they make up over one-third of the New Testament.

Today, the local church continues as the strategic base in which Christians are nurtured and from which Christians move out into the world with evangelistic and missional outreach. The local church is the bedrock of Christianity.

* * * *

Everyone "must realize that the local church is the most important part of the denomination. Here the gospel is preached. Here people either become Christians or fail to do so. If the local congregations are vital and effective, the whole church prospers."[1] Somehow The United Methodist Church has lost sight of this precept and somehow we must once again pay more than lip service to it. For the past several decades The United Methodist Church seemingly has focused its efforts on unions and new structures. This preoccupation with organization has had significant negative impact on the local church. It has been so strong and so prolonged that to question the role of the local church in respect to the general church is natural. The general agencies as well as the General Conference, perhaps without intending to do so, have sent to the members of the denomination the message that the local church is not important. Little or no time was spent by the 1988 General Conference on the direct concerns of the local church and virtually no effort was expended to determine the impact of the actions of the Conference on the local church and its members. In fact, in recent years, "the local church has been the forgotten key element."[2]

During the decades of the 1960s and 1970s, The United Methodist Church focused its attention on the major social issues of the day. This focus was at the virtual exclusion of personal spiritual growth. During this same period of time, we have watched our denominational membership decline steadily, watched the decline in Sunday school membership and attendance, and watched the decline in worship service attendance. Simultaneously, some Protestant denominations, perhaps striking a better balance between social action and personal piety, have entered significant growth periods. While the denomination's efforts were focused on issues of social action, the local churches provided The United Methodist Church with its reserves of spiritual development, faith commitment, denominational identity, and financial support. But at the same time the local congregations carried on their own development with little or no resourcing from the general or annual conference level. During this same period of time, the restructuring of the general agencies occurred with the loss of the network of individuals deeply involved with education and evangelism across the denomination. With so little emphasis on the local church, it is not unreasonable to attribute a major portion of the loss of denominational loyalty and membership to the preoccupation with non-local church concerns.

Personal Piety and Social Action

Bishop Earl G. Hunt, Jr., in his book *A Bishop Speaks His Mind*, has stated: "The impetus of our intense and wide efforts has sometimes caused United Methodism . . . to concentrate its energies and resources on the accomplishment of social objectives with a resulting neglect of personal ministries."[3] We have somehow failed to understand that our Wesleyan heritage requires our relationship with God to produce in us the desire to see those social issues that need correcting. But without developing the spiritual base of our lives, attempts at correcting the social ills commonplace in our world become simply humanism. There must be more to the Christian life than simply making our world a better place in which to live. Christ has called us to go into all the world and make disciples of all people, but we cannot even empower United Methodist local churches to perform the task in their own community. There must be a balance in the approach to personal piety and social action. In many respects there cannot be one without the other. But this balance has been lost at the general church level of our denomination and has been sharply eroded at the heart of the denomination, the local church.

Laypeople across the denomination are crying out for help in bringing their relationship to God into focus as they live their lives in the world. They want a spiritual base for their involvement in social action activities. Faith must be present to drive them out into their world to do their good works. But where is the assistance that they need and desire? Fortunately in the last several years, this cry has begun to be heard by some people beyond the local church. Our laypeople believe they are singularly unprepared to encounter their world spiritually. They have yearned for someone to provide them with the tools to deal with the world in which they live. The *Disciple* Bible study program (a program of The United Methodist Publishing House) has touched a nerve within our denomination. Our laypeople want to have a knowledge of Scripture that will enable them to hear the call of God upon their souls, to undergird their lives, and to be competent to teach Sunday school. The desire of local churches now is

to focus more and more on the central faith issues for the individual Christian and how these are dealt with in the Christian community and society. The desire is to understand more fully the Bible, the implications of Christ's teachings for daily life, and ways to express the Christian faith in worship, witness, and service.[4]

The United Methodist Church and its general agencies are called upon to address the widespread interest in the development of personal spiritual growth. "Increasingly it is recognized that preoccupation with the structures and business of the church, while necessary, has drawn United Methodists away from a central focus on Christian witness and service. Now there is the desire to renew one's personal faith and commitment."[5] This desire has been heard in the Virginia Annual Conference where in March 1986 the development of an effort designed to promote lay spiritual development began. The program was developed as a cooperative effort between the Conference Board of Laity and the staff of The Upper Room section of the General Board of Discipleship. The effort was the result of the perception that "our denomination was not answering the deep desire of our people to develop their spiritual lives as well as their physical lives."[6] The relationship between the Conference Board of Laity and The Upper Room developed from the growing awareness of the spiritual hunger of laypeople all across the church and their willingness to talk about that hunger. The pilot project in the Virginia Annual Conference became the major emphasis for the Board of Laity. "For The Upper Room, this effort directed at the *congregation* as the primary focus for spiritual direction, was a new direction in ministry."[7] The local church lay leader was a major focus of the effort since the lay leader has the capability of providing major leadership in the spiritual life of the congregation. The lay leader is aware of the hopes, pains, and longings of the laypeople of the local church.

A second key individual was the pastor, who along with the lay leader and several other laypeople composed the teams trained from each local church. These teams along with the staff members of The Upper Room developed approaches to lay spiritual development.

To undergird the program, Janice Grana, world editor of *The Upper Room* and associate general secretary of the General Board of Discipleship, established the following concepts:

—There is a restlessness for God's kingdom that includes a hunger for intimacy with God and a deep desire for a new order in our life together.

—The form of yearning or hunger is different for different people—a feeling of emptiness, a seeking for more, a search for meaning, or a restlessness for justice.

—The spiritual life is not a struggle to get from here to where God is. Instead it has to do with the claim of God upon our attention.

—Spiritual formation guides us into the heart of the world. God forms us into people who move more deeply into the pain of the world and who feel called to respond to that pain.

—The spiritual life is contemplative—a call to see God in our midst.

—The spiritual life is essentially communal. Spiritual formation involves the empowerment of our life together.[8]

The results of the lay spiritual development effort in the Virginia Annual Conference may be years in the making. However, the local churches involved noted significant results during the year-long effort. A deepening spiritual dimension was seen in the local congregations, which was developed through small groups established by the project process. As individuals involved in the effort explored ways in which the spiritual life could impact on their congregation, a deepening spiritual dimension was noted in the local congregation. The project demonstrated the action that can occur when annual conferences and general agencies of the denomination listen to the needs of the local church.

Often due to lack of assistance from denominational organizations, local churches have had to rely on themselves, seeking to solve their own problems and develop their own forms of outreach and ministry. "They learned that Annual Conferences and general agencies develop programs that often are not relevant or applicable for a particular local situation."[9] However, when efforts such as the Virginia Conference lay spiritual development program are generated from the needs of local churches, significant strides can be made. Continuing efforts are needed to equip the membership of local United Methodist churches with the necessary spiritual base to allow the people to understand *why* they are involved in social action projects.

Bishop Hunt has explicitly stated the problem:

Our critics have claimed that we have worn for more than thirty years the trappings of a spiritually arid activism accomplished too often at the expense of theological breadth and depth, philosophical and psychological maturity, and authentic devotional reflection and that our activism has become nearly monstrous, often incompletely informed, sometimes politically biased, and frequently without clear logic and dependable consistency. The emphasis has been on *doing* instead of *being*. We have produced a cacophony of loud, sometimes well-worded outcries, fashioned into resolutions often more political than religious in context, about nearly every human issue worthy of headlines. Some would say that more frequently than not the results have been distressingly poor; the church has lost depth and the body politic has not been impressed! Put another way, the controversial involvement of the church in a thousand and one social/political struggles around the globe has seemed to produce little change in the bottom line report on the human malady. Its cost effectiveness has been virtually nil.[10]

Bishop Hunt goes on to say that this analysis is not totally accurate and we agree with him. Certainly not all the social actions of The United Methodist Church are incompatible with the membership of the local congregation. But there is a clear perception among many laypeople that a gross imbalance in many of the church's social action positions has occurred. In addition, as Bishop Hunt points out, our denomination must maintain a balance between influencing society "in the holy directions of peace, justice, and righteousness . . . never forget[ting] that the core of Christian teaching has always insisted on *being* as the essential parent of effective *doing*, and our commitment to a *whole evangelism* and a *conscious cultivation of the inner spiritual life* must never be permitted to slacken."[11]

There is little doubt that many laypeople across the denomination concur in the critics' analysis of a number of the social action positions of The United Methodist Church. These laypeople firmly agree that the denomination at the general church level and to some extent at the annual conference level has become more interested in a social agenda than a spiritual agenda. The time has come to balance the two. The laypeople of our denomination seek spiritual direction in their lives in order to know what direction to take in making an impact on the world in which they live. They are no longer willing to have that agenda set for them by the members or staff of the general agencies of the church.

Worship

Worship and worship services are among the most crucial concerns of the members of local United Methodist churches. The need for vital worship experiences is not only crucial, it borders on the critical. For many United Methodists, their worship experience is provided each week in a perfunctory fashion. It has been said that the most boring hour of the week is between 11:00 A.M. and 12:00 noon on Sunday morning! The Sunday morning worship service is the point at which the hurting faithful come together to once again have their cups filled. It is here that in some respects the local church feels most profoundly the level of competence of its pastor. Not every ordained United Methodist minister needs to be a great preacher, but every one needs to be a capable preacher. A vital worship service is enhanced by great preaching, but great preaching is not necessary for a vital worship experience. People whose lives are in disarray, whose souls need refreshing, whose thoughts flee to other times and other places, whose spirits are despondent, all come to the local church at the worship hour in expectation. They come in the expectation that something transcendent will take place in their hearts and souls. They come expecting a vital worship experience. They come in the hope that their lives will be changed, that somehow God will be present to them through worship. Vital worship can and must be a part of every local United Methodist church.

Robert Wilson in *Shaping the Congregation* has stated that in the view of John Wesley, the church was the place where small groups of the faithful could meet together for worship, study, and discipline. For Wesley the church was to be inclusive. He found this evangelical emphasis to be missing from eighteenth-century Anglicanism.[12] But Wesley also was concerned about the availability of the sacraments for Methodist people. This was not a major concern in England as he encouraged his people to seek the sacraments in their local Anglican parish. However, for Americans this posed a major problem since there were virtually no ordained clergy from the Church of England in the newly independent United States. It was for this reason that Wesley ordained men for ministry in the United States. As Wilson and Harper state: "This is why an eroding of sacramental life in early Methodism or a minimizing of the sacraments today is most unfortunate."[13] For some reason, perhaps due to our early history as a denomination when ordained ministers were rare and therefore the sacraments available infrequently, we continue to deemphasize the Sacrament of the Lord's Supper in particular. A renewal of the worship experience in the local church must include a reawakened sacramental life.

Recently on the first Sunday of the month one of us attended a local church and was surprised by a different service for the Sacrament of the Lord's Supper. During this particular service many of the prayers were sung to familiar hymn tunes. The congregation had the opportunity to be part of a new worship experience. Following the early service, and throughout Sunday school and the Sunday morning fellowship hour, those who attended the early service consistently told those who had not attended this service that they were in for a surprise. For those members attending the 11:00 A.M. service, a heightened sense of expectation was produced. Later the same day at a small group meeting, as those present discussed when they felt closest to God during the past week, several specifically mentioned the Sacrament of the Lord's Supper that morning. In order to rediscover a vital worship experience, we need to rediscover the sacraments. Wilson and Harper include as a cause of our confusion in matters of faith and practice, the failure to administer the sacraments over an extended period of time.[14]

A significant major advance occurred at the 1988 General Conference when the new hymnal for the denomination was overwhelmingly endorsed by the delegates. The new hymnal has a major expansion of the hymn section and includes many new hymns from a variety of traditions. Fortunately, many hymns have had their tunes reset to more singable pitches. Other less familiar hymns have been set to familiar hymn tunes. The result has been a major improvement in the hymnody of The United Methodist Church. In addition to changes in the hymn section, the new hymnal includes the United Methodist Liturgical Psalter, a major change in the the use of the Psalms in worship over the current practice of the perfunctory responsive reading. The new Psalter provides for the use of the Psalms in worship in a variety of ways, including singing, chanting, unison reading, responsive reading, and the use of antiphons with each Psalm. With this worship resource, the local church will have an opportunity to revitalize its worship experience. The third major section of the new hymnal includes additional liturgical resources. Several different services of worship have been provided for use by the congregation. In addition, during the 1988–92 quadrennium, *The Book of Worship*, providing all approved United Methodist rituals and liturgies, will be developed. These additional resources should markedly enhance the worship experience for United Methodists.

Conference Programs

The annual conference is the basic body of the church and the link of the local churches with The United Methodist Church as a denomination. The Methodist Episcopal Church at the time of its origin chose to develop the denomination on a model that established the local congregation as a part of a connectional church. "The local congregation is not independent and is not free to act on its own."[15] In this effort the church acted to dispel any attempts at localism. For Wesley the connectionalism of the Christian church was a major conviction. Bishop Hunt speaks of his concern that the local church is existing more and more for the sake of the activities of the general church. If this is so, he muses over the question of how long it will take for the members of the local churches to begin to question the validity of the connectional system itself.[16]

In recent years, some annual conferences have begun once again to focus their attention on the local church. This action follows after a period when they too were deeply engrossed in the merger process and restructuring of conference agencies. Also during the past twenty years, some annual conferences have been appropriately concerned with ministerial pension plans and other conference housekeeping chores. Now that the conferences have essentially completed these efforts, they have been able to turn their attention to local church concerns. During this period the local churches have, in general, supported the annual conferences in these endeavors, but in recent years the churches have pressed the annual conferences for increased and improved support. The local focus is now on a different set of concerns. "The desire now is to focus more and more on the central faith issues for the individual Christian and how these are dealt with in the Christian community and society."[17] Included on this local church agenda is a desire to grow and to see the denomination grow. We know of laypeople who are tired of being associated with an organization that does not seem able to deal with its most pressing problems. As a result of this concern efforts that deal with evangelism and church growth at the conference level are being supported at least in some conferences.

For the past several years, the Virginia Annual Conference, under the leadership of Bishop Robert M. Blackburn, has intentionally acted to set the stage for local church and annual conference growth. The first of these actions was a 20-million-dollar program entitled "Revealing Christ: A Virginia Conference Program for Congregational Growth." This effort established a goal of raising 20 million dollars in funds or pledges to be paid over a three-year period. The fund-raising period was less than one year and the first report totaled $19,724,870 with nearly 25,000 families participating! These funds will be used for four actions: (1) revitalization of existing congregations (15 percent to be divided equally and returned to the districts for programs designed by the district Council on Ministries to help revitalize existing congregations), (2) growing congregations (15 percent to be used to assist existing congregations with unusual potential for growth that are at or near the end of their financial resources), (3) new congregations (55 percent to be used as a mixture of grants and loans to help establish new United Methodist congregations that have been identified), and (4) future sites, mergers, and relocations (15 percent to be used to acquire land for future church sites and to assist local churches that may want to merge and/or relocate).[18]

According to staff members of the Office of Finance and Field Service of the General Board of Global Ministries, the "Revealing Christ" campaign is the largest fund-raising program ever conducted by an annual conference. The efforts of the local churches at underwriting this effort were astonishing. Many far surpassed not only their accepted goal, but the challenge goal as well. Small as well as large churches participated in a major way. Churches in areas of the conference that are not growing in population likewise participated. Nearly three quarters of the funds raised were pledged through individual gifts donated through the local congregations. The "Revealing Christ" campaign has become a part of the lore of the conference as well as the songs and stories of the local churches. The United Methodist people of Virginia want to see churches grow, want to see the denomination grow, and are willing to participate in an annual conference program to carry out this goal.

Second, the Virginia Annual Conference has funded a special program in strategic evangelism for the 1988–89 conference year for a sum of $18,500 from conference reserve funds. This program will be used as a pilot project to determine the effectiveness of using the mass media in the work of evangelism. Numerous local churches are vying for a place in this effort.

Third, for the first time in conference history, the 1988 Virginia Annual Conference approved a quadrennial emphasis on evangelism and church growth for the 1988–92 quadrennium by an overwhelming margin. During the 1988–89 conference year a task force is developing the programmatic proposal that will be brought to the 1989 Virginia Annual Conference for approval. A grassroots approach to its design is being developed. A major effort is being made by the task force to involve as many local churches as possible in the program design. Once again a conference program has touched a nerve in the life of the local churches of the conference. When a long-felt need is met, a conference program can and will involve the local church. As Wilson and Harper indicate, not every local church will participate in conference designed programs; but when the local churches are involved in planning and programming, a substantial proportion of them will participate.[19] A key ingredient in involving local churches in annual conference programs is for the idea of the program to bubble up from below or be a top down program that touches the members of the local church in a heart-felt concern.

Local Church Structure

Although in some ways a relatively minor problem within The United Methodist Church, the local church structure of boards, councils, and committees continues to create difficulties. Many of us remember the pain we went through in the reorganization of the local church structure nearly twenty years ago. The difficulty of even trying to come to grips with a program council separate from the administrative board was difficult to grasp. Trying to define age level coordinators as something other than Sunday school superintendents was a problem. As the years have passed, the local church structure as we know it today has been refined and improved. In addition, using that structure for twenty years has resulted in its becoming a part of the life of the local church. And with passing time allowance has been made for different size churches to structure themselves in a manner that facilitates the accomplishment of the work at hand. Johnson and Waltz point out that "the Council [on Ministries] tends to obscure and delay ministries of witness, nurture, and service. For the vast majority of local United Methodist churches, this additional step is unnecessary."[20] Alan K. Waltz in *Images of the Future* states that "increased flexibility of organizational patterns will facilitate the local church's handling of its own needs and concerns."[21] We must, of course, deal with local church structure carefully. If we do not, we may find that our connectional system may be at some risk. If virtually every local church were to be structured differently, we would compound an already difficult situation of communication between the levels within the connection. Such chaos in local church structure could result in a centripetal force pulling the denomination apart. However, it should be possible to allow enough latitude in local church structure to produce a strong functioning local church. This could be accomplished as long as each local church maintained a structure in which certain key structural elements are maintained to facilitate communication with the district, annual conference, and general agencies of the church.

A significant aspect of the local church structure is the communication necessary within a connectional church. Unfortunately, communication within our denomination is less than optimal. Johnson and Waltz are explicit on this subject. "Most communication efforts underwritten by the denomination are geared to a very limited audience of the clergy and selected lay leadership. . . . The rank and file local church members and ministers have few sources for obtaining information concerning the ongoing work and direction of the church."[22] Most of what is communicated is supportive material for programs both at the general and annual conference levels. The United Methodist

Church has no general publication for clergy and laity with which to communicate in a general manner across the denomination. *Good News*, the bimonthly magazine for United Methodists, published by the Forum for Scriptural Christianity, comes the closest to a general periodical for church members. It is not an official publication of The United Methodist Church, but comes close to serving that function. Since the denomination does not publish such a periodical, much of the denominational news comes to United Methodists through unofficial sources or the lay press. In addition The United Methodist Church does not even publish its own newspaper. *The United Methodist Reporter* functions quite capably in this role, however.

The Interpreter, published by United Methodist Communications, is sent to key local church leadership and can be obtained by other laypeople through subscription. It is, however, a program journal and not a periodical for general distribution. Perhaps the most useful tool for cohesion among United Methodists would be an official, general-purpose United Methodist magazine. Such a magazine would provide a direct channel of communication to laypeople and clergy alike. It should be remembered that "lack of information often leads to suspicion, lack of interest and support. At a time when the local church has a lack of interest in the work of the organizational aspects of the denomination, the formal communication channels of the church are focused primarily on these issues."[23] For The United Methodist Church to maintain itself as a connectional church, it must improve its communication with the general membership of the denomination at the local church level.

Mission of the Local Church

Each local church must develop its own statement of mission. This is difficult, not only for local churches, but for the denomination at the general level. The 1984 General Conference established a Commission on the Mission of The United Methodist Church. This commission reported to the 1988 General Conference by submitting a mission statement for The United Methodist Church entitled "Grace upon Grace: God's Mission and Ours." This statement was accepted for study by the church during the next quadrennium. The development of mission statements is difficult, not only for local churches, but for the denomination as well. The need to clearly approve a mission statement for the church continues during the 1988–92 quadrennium. "A clear statement of the mission for the church will enable each congregation to understand its responsibility as a part of the whole and to have the broad parameters within which to work."[24] For the local church

> The development of a statement of local mission or purpose will require much soul searching. It will force people to take account of their understanding of the faith, their heritage, and the situation in which their church exists today. The completion of this task would enable the members to better understand their faith and the way that faith is lived out through the local Christian community. It would give focus to the congregation's work and enable the people to concentrate their efforts on activities and goals that are consistent with their understanding of their purpose.[25]

Difficult though it may be, the local church as well as the denomination must complete the task of preparing a statement of the mission of each, in order to know who and whose they are and in what direction they are going.

Conclusion

As we look at the local church we need to remember as Bishop Richard Wilke has pointed out, that part of our social witness deals with what is "far off" and part deals with what is "near." Those issues that are far off may be those with which church leaders have become preoccupied and are quite distant from the average member of the local church. "Issues far off are often exotic, like planting orchids. Problems at home are ordinary, like growing geraniums. But the at-homeness is where our people are, and they are going to heaven or hell in the midst of those issues. Some of our people are not getting much help in their life battles."[26] As a denomination we must provide assistance to our people as they struggle with their spiritual beings in order to know why they are driven by that faith into the world in which they live.

As a denomination we must strive to make the worship experiences of our local churches a vital force in the lives of our people. Bishop Earl Hunt states: "The raw, naked power of a gospel so revolutionary that its transcendent force is unpredictable and uncontrollable is simply absent at the eleven o'clock hour on Sunday morning in many of our churches."[27] We can no longer allow ourselves to prevent the Holy Spirit from moving our people to the depths of their souls through vital worship services. Our pastors must be given the tools to enhance our worship experiences.

We must also remember that the programs of our annual conferences and those of the general agencies of the church must speak to the heart-felt needs and concerns of our people in the local churches. For too long they have been the forgotten of our denomination. "We must trust the power of the gospel to create, at the local church level, the sort of church the gospel demands."[28] If our denomination can develop a sense of direction, our annual conferences and local churches will be able to move in tandem with the general church. If not, they will move in their own direction, focusing their efforts on those areas of mission and ministry of importance to them. Those areas will in all likelihood relate to faith and ministry issues as they are lived out in our world by our United Methodist people.

We must ensure that the local congregation is the center of The United Methodist Church. It is here that Christianity is lived out in our world. It is here that our people strive to understand what it means to be a servant people in ministry to the world around them. These are the people who provide the funds and give themselves in the leadership that undergirds all other levels of the denomination. There is nothing new in this. For two thousand years the local church has been the bedrock of Christianity. In The United Methodist Church, it will continue to be throughout our third century.

CHAPTER 6

Are We a National Church?

I therefore, a prisoner for the Lord, beg you to lead a life worthy of the calling to which you have been called, with all lowliness and meekness, with patience, forbearing one another in love, eager to maintain the unity of the Spirit in the bond of peace. There is one body and one Spirit, just as you were called to the one hope that belongs to your call, one Lord, one faith, one baptism, one God and Father of us all, who is above all and through all and in all (Eph. 4:1-6).

Ephesians is considered by many theologians to be an encyclical used as an introduction to the collected letters of Paul. We have in Scripture the letter to the Ephesians, but there may well have been the same letter to the Galatians and Corinthians for Ephesians is a summary of Paul's theology. If this theory is correct, the letter to the Ephesians (and other places) is a letter to the general church setting forth the nature of the church and individuals who comprise its membership.

In the Scripture cited above Paul begs for a living of a life worthy of the call of God. Paul paints the picture of the characteristics a person will embody when in the fellowship of the Christian Church; failure to exhibit such traits hinders the life of the church and discredits its name. The *natural* life-style of a Christian is a quality of *being* that includes humility, meekness, patience, and love—the basics of the faith. However, issuing forth from these qualities is a fifth virtue that is the "unity of the Spirit in the bond of peace." Unity is that "sacred oneness" that characterizes the true Church.

Using the metaphor of "body" for the universal Church, Paul states unity of the Spirit is possible because Christ is the head of the "body," and in him there is one common hope and goal, a world redeemed by Christ (*shalom*).

The true Church is one in the spirit because there is only one Lord, one faith, one baptism, and one God. Such a commitment supersedes local, regional, and national differences. We belong to God, we belong to one another, and we work for a world of *shalom* in which all children may have a future.

* * * *

The United Methodist Church was founded at the same time the United States became an independent nation. The church followed the nation's western movement. It was a frontier denomination that used circuit riders to follow the pioneers west. Without settled appointments the ministers found their congregations where the wisps of smoke rose above a new clearing in the trees. The church grew as the nation grew. Its theology, ritual, and organizational structures were suited to the needs of a frontier people. However, many of the struggles of the newly independent United States were also mirrored within the growing denomination. During the early period of the church, a series of five divisions occurred. In 1792, only eight years after the organization of the Methodist Episcopal Church at the Christmas Conference, James O'Kelly withdrew, taking nearly 6,500 members with him. His defection occurred over his demand that "preachers" be allowed to appeal their appointment by the bishop to the conference. His proposal was defeated by a large majority, and he withdrew with his supporters from the church. The next three separations, which involved no principles of doctrine or governance, resulted in the formation of the African Methodist Episcopal Church in 1816, the African Methodist Episcopal Zion Church in 1817, and the formation of a separate Methodist denomination in Canada.

In 1830, during the era of Jacksonian democracy, the Methodist Protestant Church was formed. It arose from the "protest against the continued exclusion of all laymen from the legislative, executive, and judicial bodies of the mother Methodist Episcopal Church."[1] The major division of the church occurred in 1844 with the separation of the Methodist Episcopal Church into northern and southern branches. "All the issues that produced the Methodist Protestant Church were ecclesiastical. Upon its consummation no serious aftereffects remained for either Church. But in 1844 the case was vastly different. The issue was not primarily ecclesiastical but social, and it permeated the entire nation."[2] During the entire 1844 General Conference, the issue of slavery was dominant, resulting in the division of the church. This division into the Methodist Episcopal Church in the northern United States and the Methodist Episcopal Church, South, in the southern United States set the stage for much of the regionalism that has subsequently occurred. Then, in 1866, the Colored Methodist Episcopal Church (now the Christian Methodist Episcopal Church) separated from the Methodist Episcopal Church, South. This was the last major division affecting the bodies that eventually came together to form The Methodist Church in 1939.

Besides being a major force in the life of the United States, The United Methodist Church is a world denomination. While about 95 percent of its members live in the United States, United Methodists can be found around the globe. These United Methodists who live outside the United States are organized into Central Conferences which function like the jurisdictions in the United States. The Central Conferences consist of annual conferences and provisional annual conferences. The latter do not have the resources to be annual conferences and are developed around mission activities. There are seven central conferences: four in Europe, two in Africa, one in the Philippines. Within these central conferences are twenty-nine annual conferences and nine provisional annual conferences.[3] These Central Conferences elect bishops who become full members of the Council of Bishops of The United Methodist Church.

In 1987, the Central Conferences had 564,783 members. Following a downward trend in membership during the 1970s, the Central Conferences have been growing since 1980. Thus about 5 percent of the denomination's members reside outside the United States. It is of interest to note that the Estonia Provisional Conference, a part of the Northern Europe Central Conference, contains the largest United Methodist church on the continent of Europe, located in Tallinn, Estonia, in the Soviet Union. Thus The United Methodist Church is not a strictly American, or national, church.

Methodism has never viewed itself in strictly national terms since from its earliest days it has had a major missionary thrust. The term "national" has two nuances: first, meaning a church confined to one country and, second, meaning a church embracing an entire nation. In the first sense of national, The United Methodist Church is not a national church since 5 percent of its members reside outside the United States and are citizens of other nations. Here we will be concerned with the second meaning of national. In both respects

The United Methodist Church is *not* a national church. Instead it has the aspects of a group of regional churches united under one umbrella. Since The United Methodist Church blankets the United States, it may be viewed as a national church, having local churches located in 97 percent of the 3,043 counties in the United States. United Methodism is rural, urban, and suburban in scope, with members of all the races represented in the American culture. Although primarily a middle-class denomination, it has members across a wide spectrum of the socio-economic fabric of our society. Unfortunately, even with a lengthy emphasis on the ethnic local church, ethnic groups comprise less than 5 percent of the denomination's total membership.[4]

The Results of Mergers

Although ninety-five years elapsed following the historic split in the Methodist Episcopal Church before the climactic merger on May 10, 1939, the result produced not a national denomination but a federation of regional churches. This occurred due to the powerful interest of the Methodist Episcopal Church, South, to maintain significant autonomy. As a result a system of geographical jurisdictions was established, in which the southern church held full sway throughout the Southeastern Jurisdiction. "When the church was reunited in 1939, the church claimed that its north-south split had been healed, yet regionalism was made an official part of the structure with the creation of five regional jurisdictions plus an overlapping one [the Central Jurisdiction] consisting of black conferences."[5] In 1968 The Methodist Church and the Evangelical United Brethren Church formed a union, bringing together a nationally constituted denomination and one that was strongly represented in the mid-Atlantic and mid-western regions of the United States. At the same time an internal union was under way in which the non-geographic Central Jurisdiction was being brought into the five geographic jurisdictions.

Over a thirty-year period, the mergers produced a denomination that appeared to be a national church. The General Conference, meeting every four years, gives the appearance of cohesion. However, the jurisdictional system essentially resulted in five regional churches. Each jurisdiction and central conference elects its own bishops. Only on two occasions has a jurisdiction elected as a bishop an elder from another jurisdiction. Although the Interjurisdictional Committee on the Episcopacy has the authority "to discuss the possibility of transfers of bishops across jurisdictional lines at the forthcoming Jurisdictional Conferences for residential and presidential responsibilities in the ensuing quadrennium,"[6] the process of such a transfer is so cumbersome that it is virtually impossible for such transfers to occur. The bishops being transferred must agree, and two bishops must be exchanged unless one jurisdiction waives the right of doing so. In addition both Jurisdictional Committees on the Episcopacy as well as both Jurisdictional Conferences must approve the plan of transfer. Although there is a Council of Bishops at the national level, each jurisdiction has its own College of Bishops. The net result is the maintenance of strong regional church structures and identity.

A variety of differences can be seen between the five jurisdictions as Warren J. Hartman has shown in *Discipleship Trends*. In confessions of faith, for example, "the North Central jurisdiction reports the highest proportionate share of professions of faith and the Southeastern jurisdiction has the lowest proportionate share of professions of faith."[7] Why do these differences occur? Do the sunbelt churches rely on gaining members through transfer of membership from the northern churches? Since they are losing members, do the frostbelt churches have to rely more heavily on new conversions? Hartman continues by noting "that more than one-half of those who are received into church membership in the North Central, Northeastern, and Western jurisdictions come on confession of faith. Slightly more than one-third of the new members in the South Central and Southeastern jurisdictions come from that source."[8] Thus significantly different dynamics appear to be at work in the various geographic jurisdictions that represent the people of different areas of the country.

Jurisdictional differences were clearly discernible in the positions of delegates to the 1988 General Conference. The Office of Research of the General Council on Ministries published a survey of delegates in February 1988, which did not provide data broken down by jurisdiction. *The United Methodist Reporter*, however, conducted several surveys prior to the 1988 General Conference.

The data obtained through these surveys was broken down by jurisdiction. The three issues of November 13, 1987, March 4, 1988, and April 1, 1988, dealt with the issues to come before the 1988 General Conference.

Delegates were asked to list in order of importance the three most important issues to come before the conference. "In none of the church's five geographic U. S. jurisdictions did the collective regional ordering of issues exactly match the first 10 topics in the denomination-wide ranking."[9] For example, the number-one ranking priority in the North Central Jurisdiction was membership, growth, and evangelism, while this issue ranked no higher than eighth in the Southeastern Jurisdiction. The twelfth issue in ranking denomination-wide was the change in the number of bishops. The two jurisdictions most interested in such a change—the Southeastern and South Central—placed these tenth and ninth respectively. *The United Methodist Reporter* poll concerning the major issue of homosexuality coming before the conference demonstrated significant jurisdictional differences. From the Western Jurisdiction, only 34.8 percent of the delegates responding to the poll believed that the United Methodist Social Principles statement declaring the practice of homosexuality incompatible with Christian teaching should be maintained. From the Southeastern Jurisdiction, 95.7 percent felt that it should be retained. Of the total respondents, 77.7 percent would maintain the statement.[10] Thus the delegates' position differed significantly on this issue. On the issue of the development of a new hymn book, there were likewise differences noted between jurisdictions. "Delegates from the 2.9-million-member Southeastern Jurisdiction recorded the weakest positive response on whether the proposed hymnal could be used 'happily and effectively' in their congregations. Southeasterners also registered the highest negative opinions about the psalter and rituals in the proposed book. . . .

"But comments from delegates in the 525,000-member Western Jurisdiction indicated satisfaction with alternative rituals and inclusive language."[11]

Another opportunity to determine the stance of individuals within The United Methodist Church occurred following the writing of the "Houston Declaration." This document was produced by forty-eight United Methodist pastors at a meeting

December 14-15, 1987, in Houston, Texas. These pastors spoke to three issues: "(1) the primacy of Scripture; (2) the nature and name of the one God, Father, Son, and Holy Spirit; (3) the high and holy character of ordained ministry."[12] This document was mailed to all United Methodist pastors and all local church lay leaders for whom an address could be obtained, and they were asked to return a postal card indicating their level of support for the Declaration. Nearly 30 percent of those surveyed responded. The lowest number of positive responses was tabulated from the Western Jurisdiction. Here pastors appointed to the local church responded positively only 55 percent of the time. But lay leaders responded positively in 88 percent of cases. Pastors appointed beyond the local church recorded a 43 percent positive response. The jurisdiction total was 62 percent positive. The highest positive response rate was from the Southeastern Jurisdiction. Pastors appointed to the local church responded positively in 95 percent of cases. Lay leaders responded positively 97 percent of the time, while pastors appointed beyond the local church registered an 83 percent positive vote. The jurisdiction total was 95 percent positive.[13] Clearly there is a difference in how these three key issues are perceived in the jurisdictions.

Our contention is that there appear to be significant differences between the jurisdictions within The United Methodist Church. This is particularly apparent in regard to major social issues, such as homosexuality, and in regard to theological issues such as the Trinity and primacy of Scripture. These differences seem to be direct outgrowths of the series of unions that have been accomplished by the denomination. The unions have produced five regional churches which have to some degree pursued their own agenda. The result is a significant amount of disagreement at the level of the General Conference and the general agencies of the church. A major effort needs to be mounted in the future to allow the denomination to recover and coalesce around a middle ground of Wesleyan theology.

The Seven Churches of Methodism

The geographical jurisdictions may not be the only regional system within The United Methodist Church. Wilson and Willimon have published a monograph entitled *The Seven Churches of Methodism,* in which they write about the regionalism within The United Methodist Church. They state that regionalism is rarely discussed within the denomination for fear that unity will not be maintained. The whole issue of unity is one that followed the 1844 division of the Methodist Episcopal Church. Bishop John M. Moore in *The Long Road to Methodist Union* defined union and unity as follows: "Unity is always spiritual; union may be mechanical. Union is proper and desirable only when it leads to unity."[14]

As we discuss regionalism in the church, we need to keep in mind · that unity and union are not necessarily the same. Somehow it may be that we need to consider that regionalism is not necessarily a threat to national programs and funds. Perhaps failing to understand regionalism within the church poses the largest threat. If we refuse to consider our regional differences, we may find that we will not mobilize our resources to deal with substantial issues in the various geographic areas of the nation. For as we saw in the preceding section there are differences of opinion in the important issues of the various jurisdictions of the church. Likewise, Wilson and Willimon have discovered differences in the seven regions into which they divided the denomination. "We contend that the United Methodist Church is not one church, but seven. These 'churches' have much in common but these are also significant sectional variations. To understand Methodism, the tensions and conflicts within the church and why it functions as it does, one must understand regional differences."[15] The Yankee church is defined as New England plus the Troy Conference in New York, but without western Connecticut, which is a part of the New York Conference. The Industrial Northeastern Church includes the United Methodist churches in the states of New York (including western Connecticut, but excluding the Troy Conference), Pennsylvania, New Jersey, Delaware, Maryland, and West Virginia. The Church South is all of southeastern United States from the Atlantic seaboard through Louisiana. The Midwest Church, Methodism's heartland, is bordered by Ohio on the east, Canada on the north, the Dakotas, Nebraska and Kansas on the west, and the Ohio River and the southern boundaries of Missouri and Kansas on the south. The Southwest Church consists of Texas,

Arkansas, Oklahoma, and New Mexico. The Frontier Church is made up of the states of Colorado, Wyoming, Montana, and Utah. The Western Church covers the west coast of the United States, including Alaska and Hawaii.

These seven regions do not coincide with the five jurisdictions of the church. However the two maps overlap considerably. The Yankee Church and the Industrial Northeastern Church together comprise the Northeastern Jurisdiction. The Church South is the Southeastern Jurisdiction plus Louisiana. The Midwest Church is the North Central Jurisdiction plus the northern half of the South Central Jurisdiction. The Southwest Church is the southern portion of the South Central Jurisdiction. The Frontier Church plus the Western Church make up the Western Jurisdiction. Thus although divided into seven parts instead of five, these geographic areas in the study of Wilson and Willimon do have remarkably different interests and positions on the various issues within the denomination. These differences lend credence to the idea that The United Methodist Church is a federation of regional churches, not a cohesive national body.

For example, The Yankee Church is the weakest section of the church. It is an area where Methodism has never been particularly strong, having been settled early by individuals who were adherents to other denominations. In addition a large number of Roman Catholics have migrated into the area over the years. Wilson and Willimon point out that the area, through the Boston University School of Theology, has had a significant impact on Methodism for some years. This influence has waned during the last half of the twentieth century. "The most significant aspect of the Yankee Church has been its decline since 1970."[16] From 1970 to 1982, church membership fell by 17.5 percent. In addition there was a drastic decrease in average Sunday school attendance. As a consequence of this major decline in the strength of the church in New England, Wilson and Willimon report a pessimistic attitude in the Yankee Church. They report that as the decline has occurred, ideology and clerical issues have become predominant:

> The indications are that Yankee Methodism is facing a crisis of serious proportions. Never strong the church's 18 percent membership decrease in a dozen years borders on the catastrophic. Because the church school has been a major source of new members, the drop

of 49 percent in average attendance does not bode well for the future. Giving attention to internal matters such as annual conference boundaries or restricting admission to the ministry does not address the basic theological and congregational issues. The immediate future will determine not only whether New England Methodism will continue to be a voice in the region but even a significant part of Methodism.[17]

The Industrial Northeastern Church historically was the strong-hold of the Methodist Episcopal Church. In the past, many of the great churches of Methodism were located in this area. As the white population moved to the suburbs and the Black population migrated north to the great cities, a significant decline in Methodism occurred in this area. Methodist churches were singularly unsuccessful at winning the allegiance of those Blacks who moved north and settled in the inner cities. "One of the most significant aspects of the congregations of the Northeast has been the inability to attract blacks to their membership."[18] Like the Yankee Church (also a part of the Northeastern Jurisdiction), the Industrial Northeastern Church has decreased its membership by 22 percent during the same twelve-year period and its Sunday school has declined by more than half! The decline of the large downtown churches in this area has had a major impact on the denomination as a whole. Wilson and Willimon report that in this area Methodism is in great danger of becoming a minor denomination, certainly a far cry from its halcyon days.

> The industrial Northeast has traditionally had the self-image of being the pace-setting region for the denomination, both theologically and programmatically. This was the case in the past, but is no longer true as Methodism enters its third century. The church is doing poorly in the urban centers. It is recruiting few blacks and does not seem to be able to reach the poor; a particular scandal for a people who were born in the Wesleyan vision of reaching all orders of society with the Gospel.[19]

The Church South and the Southwest Church comprise most of the area in which the Methodist Episcopal Church, South, had its greatest strength. With union in 1939, the southern church was careful not to be swallowed up by the northern church. This was accomplished through the creation of the geographic jurisdictions. As Bishop Moore wrote in *The Long Road to Methodist Union*, the characteristics of the various sections of the country are sufficiently different as to create varied human values and characteristics.[20] These differences have continued to be evident in the Church South. Here Methodism has a tendency to continue to be traditional in both style and theology. The denomination is relatively strong in the South with a less than 4 percent decrease in membership during the twelve-year period studied. The Sunday school declined by about 25 percent during the same period. In this region, the church is in a state of stability rather than of growth. The authors expect the church in the South to play an increasingly greater role in the denomination as a whole, particularly since about one-third of all United Methodists reside in this region. There is a strong spirit of optimism found among church members here.

The Midwest Church is still a strong force in the denomination. The merger of 1968 added further strength as the Evangelical United Brethren Church was a significant force in this region. Only the South has more members than the Midwest Church. During the twelve-year period studied, this region lost only about 10 percent of its members and the Sunday school declined by a little over one-third. "Midwestern Methodism has and continues to be traditional at the grass roots. The leadership, particularly the clergy, have the image of being avant-garde, of being in the forefront of social change."[21] Due to the large area covered geographically by this church, a strong regional identity has not been developed. Without an assembly center or major jurisdictional programs, plus its sheer size, the Midwest Church is composed primarily of a collection of annual conferences.

The Southwest Church represents the only region of the denomination that has exhibited growth in the 1970–1982 period. Self-confidence and optimism are found in this section of Methodism, since members of local churches expect the church to be effective both in the present and on into the future. This region has nearly half of the largest churches in the denomination. It is here that a major influx of Hispanic immigrants has occurred in recent years, but unfortunately the church has not found an effective means of ministering to these individuals.

The Frontier Church is quite small with only about four hundred local churches within four states. Church membership dropped about 17 percent during the study period, but Sunday school attendance plummeted by over 40 percent. A major factor in this region is the strength of the Mormon Church. Because of it, all other Christian denominations are in the minority. "The conditions in the Frontier Church seem to have produced a hardy breed of Methodist people who minister in a difficult and sometimes hostile environment."[22]

The Western Church has trended down through the study period even though this region of the United States has grown dramatically. As a result Methodism is rather weak in this region. At the end of 1982, there were only 425,000 members in the Western Church, resulting from a 23 percent loss over the twelve years. In the Sunday school, the membership has been cut in half! "At some point the Western Church seems to have decided to drop the church school as a vibrant part of church life."[23] This area has been perceived to be the most liberal area of the denomination, both socially and theologically. Although there may be a liberal leadership, at least some of the churches have maintained a more traditional approach due primarily to the region having had strong elements of the Methodist Episcopal Church, South. The southern churches have continued to be somewhat more traditional, as have some of the Evangelical United Brethren churches. "The Western Church is something of an enigma. . . . The period immediately ahead will determine if the Western Church will continue to be a force in the region and a vital part of the denomination."[24]

Even though the denomination has attempted to ignore regional differences, such differences play a significant role in the function of The United Methodist Church. "These differences may be so potentially divisive that the church, remembering the struggles of the past, prefers to ignore them."[25] It should be remembered that regional differences are not necessarily bad. They allow the church to have an impact on the major issues in a particular area. The various parts of the church have the opportunity to learn from one another. However, regional differences can be destructive if they are ignored by the church, particularly when actions are taken by the church under the mistaken notion that The United Methodist Church is homogeneous.

Issues of Fairness

Although The United Methodist Church attempts to portray a unified and national presence, in some regions of the church there is a perception of a lack of fairness in the selection of the staff and members of the general agencies. The various locations of the general agencies are an outgrowth of the merger process within the denomination. It is not unnatural that to a significant extent these agencies reflect the regional character of their predecessors. For example, part of the 1939 union was an agreement that a major board would be located in the northern area of the United States, and another major board would be located in the South. This resulted in the education board being located in Nashville and the mission agency being located in New York. The 1968 union included maintaining United Methodist offices in Dayton, Ohio, the location of the Evangelical United Brethren Church.

There appears to be a significant regional preponderance in the selection of the staff members of the agencies. Wilson and Willimon have reported that "the agencies tend to be representative of certain regions. While the boards of managers are selected on the basis of regional membership, a large proportion of the executive and professional staff who are the key leaders in these agencies are from the north and the midwest."[26] These authors examined the annual conference membership of the 147 ordained ministers serving the key staff positions of the agencies and discovered that two-thirds are members of annual conferences located in the North and Midwest. The perception of an unfair distribution in key staff positions has been a significant element in the effort to establish tenure for the elected staff members, either clergy or lay. The Southeastern and South Central Jurisdictions clearly perceive that they have been discriminated against in the selection of key board staff. The debate has been waged over the issue of accountability, but the feelings in the southern tier of annual conferences run much deeper. Some of this resentment is a carry-over from prior to the 1939 merger.

A part of this perception of lack of sensitivity to southern concerns was partially addressed by the 1988 General Conference. The two southern jurisdictions have long felt that they were inadequately represented in the Council of Bishops. Prior to the 1988 General Conference, provision had been made for 46 episcopal areas in the United States. Of these, 45.6 percent of the bishops were located in the Southeastern and South Central Jurisdictions. Legislative action at the 1988 General Conference resulted in a change in the method of deployment of bishops, resulting in the opportunity for three jurisdictions—Southeastern, South Central, and North Central—to divide a total of four episcopal areas. Two, Birmingham and Atlanta, are in the Southeastern Jurisdiction; one, Dallas–Fort Worth, is in the South Central Jurisdiction; and one, Indiana, is in the North Central.[27] Obviously, there is widespread interest in dividing the three episcopal areas in the Southeastern and South Central Jurisdictions. There is less interest at present of doing so in the North Central Jurisdiction. With a total of 49 bishops, the two southern jurisdictions would provide 49 percent of the members of the Council of Bishops. In the case of all four areas dividing, with a total of 50 bishops, the Southeastern and South Central Jurisdictions would make up 48 percent. This is significant when it is realized that according to the *1987 General Minutes of the Annual Conferences of The United Methodist Church*, the Southeastern and South Central Jurisdictions comprise 52.7 percent of the total membership of the denomination.[28] The result of this General Conference legislation has been to assuage the feelings of the southern areas of the United States, since it provides a significant improvement in the deployment of bishops and at the same time improves the equity of representation for these geographic areas of the denomination.

A National Headquarters

As a result of mergers, The United Methodist Church has developed a decentralized system of general agency management. This system is visible through the multiple locations of denominational agencies. Having developed a regionalized placement of these facilities, it is not surprising that a certain regionalism continues. It is also not surprising that there is a desire on the part of the key elected staff members to remain in their positions for long periods of time. There is simply no place to go unless they relocate in another regional center of The United Methodist Church.

Fifty years ago, at the time of the 1939 merger, locating agencies in various cities had a strong rationale. But as time has passed, the strength that could be provided to the church by a central denominational headquarters became more obvious. Certain of the accountability issues in regard to elected staff members may become a moot point as career moves could be made between agencies without resulting in personal relocation. Tenure rules would have little force if individuals, lay and clergy, could build careers within the structures of the church rather than a single agency. A central rather than a diffuse United Methodist Church Center could provide the glue to hold together the separate geographical jurisdictions or the "Seven Churches of Methodism." Regionalism has a certain appeal, but at the same time an administrative and program center would help, in the words of Bishop Moore, to provide not only union but unity as well.

Summary

Even though roughly 95 percent of United Methodists reside in the United States, the denomination is not strictly speaking a national church. Although it is international in its scope, it performs the service of a national denomination in the United States. Due to its history of divisions and reunifications, The United Methodist Church has developed a decidedly regional appearance. This appearance has been emphasized by the jurisdictional system, the regional election of bishops, and regional control of the key staff members of general agencies. The 1988 General Conference addressed some of these issues in a positive manner from the viewpoint of the two southern jurisdictions. The development of a denominational center in place of the regional centers that grew out of the mergers of the predecessor denominations would accelerate the centripetal impetus generated by the 1988 General Conference.

CHAPTER 7

Where's the CEO?

Like an eagle that stirs up its nest,
that flutters over its young,
spreading out its wings, catching them,
bearing them on its pinions,
the Lord alone did lead him.

(Deut. 32:11-12*a*)

Moses is saying good-bye to the Hebrew people; he will not lead them into the Promised Land; Joshua will do this. Moses in his farewell address is saying that God's nature is like an eagle.

Nothing is more interesting about an eagle than its nesting habits. Eagles build their nests on high cliffs and tall trees in the high mountains. The nest is called an aerie and is usually five to seven feet in depth and width, yet the female eagle lays the eggs in a four-inch indentation. After the eaglets are hatched, both parents feed, care for their other needs, and give them flying lessons. At first, when the eaglets fly out of the nest and over the cliff their wings are not strong enough to carry them back to the nest, so just at the right moment one of the parent eagles will fly with outstretched wings underneath the eaglet and carry it back to the nest. This will be repeated over and over until the day the eaglet's wings are strong enough to return on its own to the nest.

It is then that the parent eagles get into the aerie and with their strong beaks stir up the nest so that eaglets will not have a warm, comfortable, safe, secure home when they return. It is time for them to soar on the wind currents, to develop body strength so that they can become the eagles they were created to be.

Moses said God is like an eagle that stirs up its nest. Many of the inner and outer stirrings we feel and read about in our world, our church, and our individual lives come from God. God is saying it is time to get out of the nest and become what we are created to be, to risk, to adventure, to grow.

This chapter may be only the stirrings of the writers. If so, thank you for letting us share them with you. On the other hand, if this is

God stirring the nest, may we know it and move out and soar on the wind currents of the Holy Spirit.

* * * *

In the previous chapter we wrote of the regionalism prevalent within The United Methodist Church. Although having many characteristics of a national church, the denomination does not have a national headquarters. Likewise it does not have a national executive branch of government. The General Conference is clearly the legislative branch of the church and the Judicial Council provides the judiciary function. The general boards and agencies have certain executive aspects, but not for the church as a whole. The purpose of the General Council on Ministries "is to facilitate the Church's program life as determined by the General Conference."[1] But again, it does not have a significant executive function. The Constitution of The United Methodist Church establishes the Council of Bishops which is to "plan for the general oversight and promotion of the temporal and spiritual interests of the entire Church."[2] The bishops are granted residential and presidential supervision in the Jurisdictional Conferences within which they have been elected. However, the Constitution does not provide for either bishops or laypeople to have residential or presidential duties for the general church. There is simply no chief executive officer of The United Methodist Church!

Leaders vs. Managers

Following the 1968 union of The Methodist Church and the Evangelical United Brethren Church, The United Methodist Church decided to establish the general church structure on a corporate model. As pointed out by Deal and Kennedy in their book, *Corporate Cultures*, every organization has rites and rituals of corporate life. They essentially define leaders as heroes:

> If values are the soul of the culture, then heroes personify those values and epitomize the strength of the organization. . . . The hero is the great motivator, the magician, the person everyone will count on when things get tough. . . . Heroism is a leadership component

that is all but forgotten by modern management. . . . Managers run
institutions; heroes create them. . . .
    Managers are disciplined; heroes are playful and appreciate the
value of "hoopla." . . .
    The management ethic has to do with order, procedure, and fitting
square pegs into square holes. Heroes defy order in pursuing their
vision.[3]

Leadership is a difficult commodity to find, particularly since the
term is so amorphous that everyone has a different definition for it.
Deal and Kennedy raise an interesting point when they build their
definition around the concept of heroism. Where in The United
Methodist Church are the heroes? Where are the national leaders
of our denomination?

    James McGregor Burns writes of the five characteristics of
transforming leadership, a style of leadership that may fit the
leadership requirements of The United Methodist Church. First, he
writes of the need for transforming leadership to be collective.
Leadership is collective, not in the sense that it is provided by a
committee, but that there must be interaction between the leader
and the follower. This concept allows for the coalescing of the
leader and followers into an effective working organization.
Second, he states that to be effective, a leader must not be afraid of
conflict. Such a leader is not paralyzed by needing to operate in a
consentual style that always seeks agreement or unity. An effective
transforming leader will take the initiative. Third, transforming
leadership is causative, that is, a person who makes things happen.
Fourth, this form of leadership is morally purposeful. An effective
leader provides direction and helps choose goals as well as values.
The transforming leader joins with the followers in defining the
purpose of the organization. In this manner the transforming leader
develops and motivates those who are being led. Fifth, this form of
leadership is elevating since it asks for sacrifice from those who
follow, since it cannot promise certain desired results to those who
are led.[4]

    How then can The United Methodist Church develop trans-
forming leaders? The task is exceedingly difficult since

we are faced with a crisis in leadership and in confidence from church
members. . . .
    Strong leadership has been criticized so persistently in the church,

even to the point of branding it pathological in nature, that only those who carefully "play the rules of the game" and become adept at the "game of process" are looked upon as "safe leaders." There is little chance for risk and vision in such leadership.[5]

Willimon and Wilson address this issue when they compare and contrast managers and leaders. These authors state a commonly held truth when they write that every institution needs both managers and leaders. Clearly there are routine tasks that require the expertise of managers, but Willimon and Wilson believe that The United Methodist Church as an organization has become dominated by managers. Managers, they write, are interested in the maintenance of institutions. In our denomination too much effort is going into the process of maintaining the organization with the appropriate types of people, instead of determining what is actually being accomplished. "Our church is overmanaged and underled. The rules are being followed, but there is no vision. Managers may be efficient in keeping the organizational wheels turning smoothly. However, leaders help people to see and to move toward significant goals."[6] They further state that our official church rhetoric is of bold leadership, but what we have in reality is "control and maintenance of the institutional status quo at all levels of the connectional structure and suppression of alternative points of view."[7]

As we look at leadership in The United Methodist Church, we clearly realize that our denomination is not alone in this problem. There is a general feeling of remoteness and lack of responsiveness in most large organizations.[8] Since this is a universal perception, it is, therefore, that much more difficult for the church to deal with the situation. Bishop Richard B. Wilke has stated that the denominational leadership must center its efforts on vital tasks. He believes that our times call for dramatic, decisive leadership across all levels of the denomination.[9] Therefore, "the challenge at every level of The United Methodist Church is to find strong, creative, and sensitive leadership, who will find in The United Methodist Church a constituency ready and willing to support its efforts."[10]

Bishop R. Sheldon Duecker has raised several significant issues concerning decision making. One of the most telling arguments is that there is no central decision-making center of authority in The United Methodist Church. This absence of a center of power and authority simply confuses the membership of the church. Since there is no formal executive branch in the denomination, there is no means of enforcing legislative decisions made by the General Conference. Local churches that wish to do so can simply neglect to carry out the mandates of the General Conference, thus passively rejecting actions with which they disagree.[11] The same thing can occur in the case of the general agencies which will be dealt with later.

A major issue, then, revolves around the leadership role in the denomination. What should be the role of individuals vs. groups? Duecker states:

> The term "leader" usually refers to an individual. United Methodist polity has been designed so that leadership is not in the hands of individuals, but of groups. At the general church level these groups include the Council of Bishops, General Council on Ministries, General Council on Finance and Administration, and other agencies. While most agencies have staff who exert much influence, no person is or would be authorized to be *the* leader for the entire United Methodist denomination.[12]

We will review the leadership roles of several of these groups.

Bishops and the Council of Bishops

Since its beginning, Methodism in America has had the office of general superintendent, or bishop, as a key position in the connectional system. There are some who believe that United Methodist bishops may be the most powerful church officials in the Protestant denominations in the United States. The power of the bishops has been controversial since the beginning. The formation of the Methodist Protestant Church in 1830 occurred partially over this question. It even had some impact on the decision of the Methodist Episcopal Church to split into northern and southern halves since a part of the debate centered on whether or not the General Conference had the authority to order a bishop to cease to function.[13] In addition, at the 1976 General Conference, there was a serious attempt to discontinue the life tenure of United Methodist bishops. This effort failed but there still continues to be some sentiment to move to term appointments for bishops.

The United Methodist Church has brought together in one

person the two functions of bishop and general superintendent. The superintendency gives the individual significant responsibility for overseeing the temporal affairs of the church, particularly at the annual conference level. At the same time the United Methodist bishop is an ordained elder of the church and by consecration to the office has become a spiritual head of the church as well. Upon assignment to an area, a bishop becomes the chief executive officer of the annual conference or conferences over which he or she presides. As such, the bishop oversees the spiritual and temporal affairs of the annual conference. However, there is no provision for such a specific function for a bishop at the level of the general church. The denomination-wide executive function is exercised by the Council of Bishops. *The Discipline* states: "The Council of Bishops is thus the collegial expression of episcopal leadership in the Church and through the Church into the world. The Church expects the Council of Bishops to speak to the Church and from the Church to the world."[14]

Bishops do have a certain amount of power, both personally, and as a Council. There is no question that having been elected to the episcopacy with life tenure relieves the bishops of other concerns that could impede their ability to accomplish the tasks set forth in the Constitution and *The Discipline*. Since the bishop's term does not expire, only retirement effectively removes the bishop from the direct presidential, general church, and residential responsibilities. Only one bishop has ever been removed for cause and only five bishops have ever resigned the office. Even following retirement, bishops continue to be active but without vote in the Colleges of Bishops and the Council of Bishops. They are available to the church for both their counsel and their active participation in the affairs of the denomination. At the end of the nineteenth century, the office of bishop was a powerful one. Through the intervening years, the power of the bishops has waned. "As a result of these changes bishops have become more and more limited to symbolic leadership, while functional leadership has been assigned to more and more groups."[15] Some of the most influential groups are now the general agencies of the church.

The Council of Bishops still has the potential to provide the transforming leadership that the church requires. This group of individuals has the unique situation of having continuity of experience. With life tenure and continued involvement in their respective College of Bishops and the Council of Bishops following retirement, bishops have the opportunity to provide a type of experience to the denomination that is virtually unavailable elsewhere. The election of bishops gives them a status unrivaled by other clergy or laypeople within the church. They must be approved by their peers and elected at the Jurisdictional or Central Conference by both the clergy and lay leadership assembled. The 1964 report: "Study of the General Superintendency of The Methodist Church," stated, "It is suggested that the Council of Bishops should accept a broader responsibility for leadership in the church as a whole." Bishop Duecker believes that the study is applicable today.[16] To meet its objectives will require bishops to be transforming leaders.

Although the bishops have considerable power, it is circumscribed by several factors. One of these is clearly the ability of the individual bishop to lead, not manage. Power flows from leadership, not managerial or administrative skills. The latter are important and certainly assist the bishop in the performance of the duties of general superintendent. Of more importance is the bishops' ability to provide spiritual and temporal leadership that leads to a willing servant ministry on the part of both laity and clergy alike. This form of leadership gives the individual bishop all the power needed to effectively direct the spiritual and temporal affairs of an annual conference.

One of the most important factors that circumscribes the power of the bishops is "peer pressure as the bishops counsel with each other. All the bishops are aware that their actions are being monitored not only by the constituents in their areas but also by episcopal colleagues."[17] There is a certain unfortunate aspect to this factor. If the bishops bow to collective peer pressure, then the real possibility of "group think" occurs. Failure to dissent with their colleagues may, therefore, stifle the lonely, prophetic voice within the Council of Bishops. Laypeople hope and pray that our bishops seek the counsel of God, and not one another, for their direction.

Fortunately, the third factor that circumscribes the power of bishops is their servant ministry. These individuals have spent their lives in the service of God and humanity. With that as their background, it is their obvious desire to serve the church they love and to dedicate their lives to its mission and ministry. On occasion, however, they allow this factor to interfere with the transforming leadership required today.

General Council on Ministries

The development of the General Council on Ministries was a direct outgrowth of the 1968 union. In the Evangelical United Brethren Church, the Council on Administration had functioned on a national level with its focus on accountability, coordination, and the effective performance of the other agencies of the denomination. This organization had a full-time staff and some authority over the other agencies. For a relatively small denomination, it worked surprisingly well, particularly since all the general agencies of the church were in the same location. The Methodist Church had a vaguely similar organization—the Coordinating Council, whose main function was to reduce tension between the other agencies of the denomination. Therefore the Uniting Conference of 1968 established a Program Council, which was later refined at the 1972 General Conference, becoming General Council on Ministries.

The tasks of the General Council on Ministries as established by *The Discipline* are "to encourage, coordinate, and support the general agencies as they serve on behalf of the denomination."[18] This function had a great deal of appeal when initially instituted. A large complex organization needs an agency to perform these important functions. But as the General Council on Ministries was designed, it has no serious executive function. The result has been that "the concept of the Council on Ministries as established in the new denomination was and remains essentially flawed."[19] At the national level, it has directed its attention to administrative and organizational concerns rather than to efforts that would materially enhance the programming function of the general church agencies. Interestingly, the General Conference turned over some of the authority of the Council of Bishops to the General Council on Ministries. Some of the key functions previously under the purview of the Council of Bishops are now carried out by the General Council on Ministries.

Johnson and Waltz in *Facts and Possibilities* state that the Council on Ministries concept as developed had great potential. "However, it has become an organization that is devoting much of its interest and energies to directing and controlling the administrative aspects of the life of the denomination on each level rather than on the clear planning and advocacy for and development of the outreach and ministry opportunities."[20] But, the reason the General Council on Ministries is so involved in administrative activity of the program agencies may simply be because there is no other agency in the structure of The United Methodist Church to perform it. That it is less than effective in this role should come as no surprise since, unlike the Evangelical United Brethren Council on Administration, the other general boards and agencies are scattered through other cities. Since there is no other executive agency in the denomination, the General Council on Ministries, by default, has attempted to fill the void.

General Agencies

The question must be raised as to whether or not the general agencies of the denomination can effectively fill the executive function for the church. They have the staff and funding to serve as departments within an executive branch of government for the denomination, but they currently operate without supervision. As quoted earlier in chapter 3, Bishop Earl G. Hunt, Jr., has clearly stated that the general agencies must fulfill their responsibilities faithfully as set forth by the General Conference. Their failure to do so even when displeased by the actions of the General Conference "perplexes the church and destroys the credibility of boards and agencies when directors or staffs, albeit subtly, work in behalf of positions contrary to those taken by General Conference."[21]

A clear example is the action of the executive committee of the General Board of Church and Society to call on United Methodists to join a general boycott of California table grapes.[22] This vote occurred only sixty days following the action of the 1988 General Conference rejecting such a boycott, with 556 delegates voting against the proposed boycott and 328 voting in favor of it.[23] Yet within just two months the executive committee of the General Board of Church and Society was moving to nullify the action of the only body that can speak for The United Methodist Church.

An editorial in the July 8, 1988, issue of *The United Methodist Reporter* confirms Bishop Hunt's statement above as follows, "Coming so soon after General Conference rejected a similar boycott, the Church and Society action promotes confusion about United Methodism's stance on this boycott. . . .

Many members of our church understandably will wonder why a United Methodist general agency is advocating a position that the General Conference rejected just a few weeks previously."[24] Indeed this vote by the executive committee of the General Board of Church and Society is exactly why The United Methodist Church requires a strong chief executive officer.

A Chief Executive Officer

The United Methodist Church at the national level functions as a group of competing fiefdoms. Every general agency of the denomination appears to be autonomous. As noted above, at least some of the general agencies function as if they were not responsible to the General Conference. With the decline in power and prestige of the Council of Bishops, and with the General Council on Ministries now having some of the authority that formerly rested with the Council of Bishops, there is ample requirement for a chief executive officer of The United Methodist Church.

The point is made by Bishop Richard B. Wilke in his book *And Are We Yet Alive?* He tells two stories, each of which is directly applicable to this issue. The first is as follows:

> Immediately after I was consecrated a bishop, a friend came to see me. He was president and CEO of a major corporation, a marvelous Christian, and a great churchman. He went right to the point; he said, "Dick, any large company that has a track record like The United Methodist Church, whose charts show steady decline, would have been called on the carpet long ago. The board of directors would have demanded emergency meetings, and the corporate executives would have been held accountable. Consultants would have been brought in. Heads would roll. It would not be business as usual."[25]

Bishop Wilke's second story is similar to the first:

Recently I was asked by a lay friend, "Who is your boss?" I thought
for a moment, then pointed my finger skyward. "God?" he said,
surprised. "I guess so," I replied. "No one else ever asks me to report
on the seven hundred and ninety-one congregations in Arkansas."[26]

These two stories clearly point out that there is no one who can be
held accountable for The United Methodist Church at the national
level. Intent as we have been on developing our denomination on a
corporate model, we have simply failed to develop an executive
function. Without it there is no one to be held accountable.

In Bishop Wilke's first story there is no one for his friend to hold
accountable for the failures of the church. Whose head could roll?
How can the General Conference be held accountable? The delegates
are elected every four years and serve effectively for a twelve-day
period. As every corporate executive or United Methodist pastor has
discovered, it is virtually impossible to hold a committee accountable.
Therefore the bishops in the Council of Bishops are a poor choice for
accountability for the church. Each of them can and should be held
accountable for their assigned area, but that is far different from
holding the whole council accountable for the church. The General
Council on Ministries does not have the power inherent in its charter
to hold the general agencies accountable. Each general agency must
be accountable for its portion of the national function, but it is difficult
for a committee composed of directors of each agency to be held
accountable to the entire church. Bishop Wilke states that someone
must hold the bishops accountable, and he provides a variety of
possible mechanisms, none of which would be entirely appropriate.

In the second story, Bishop Wilke clearly points out the problem
when he says there is no one other than God to whom he, as a bishop
of The United Methodist Church, is directly responsible. It is here
that a chief executive officer of the denomination assisted by the
executive departments (general agencies) of the church would be able
to provide the transforming leadership required. A modest proposal
has previously been made in this direction. Although the 1968
General Conference endorsed a proposal that a bishop be elected as
the full-time secretary of the Council of Bishops, this constitutional
amendment failed to be enacted. A revival and revision of this
proposal could suggest the election of one bishop to serve as president
of The United Methodist Church with full authority to serve as the
chief executive officer of the denomination. The term served could be

four years with the right of succession for a maximum of two terms. If the serving bishop were not eligible for retirement, reassignment to an area within the original jurisdiction would occur.

Other possibilities for an effective chief executive officer will come readily to mind as the issue is considered. Clearly anyone in The United Methodist Church could be eligible to serve in this elected full-time position. Bishop, clergy, or laity could all be considered. Logically with such a position would come the full range of an executive branch of The United Methodist Church. To be effective, a national United Methodist Church Center would need to be developed in order that effective leadership and administrative activity could be carried out.

Conclusion

The United Methodist Church has not demonstrated since the 1968 union an ability to effectively operate as a church with a national and international scope. At the national level general agencies seem to function autonomously. There is no effective means of accountability within the denomination. As Bishop Wilke has stated with pithy candor, "Remember, as sick as we are, superficial cosmetics won't suffice."[27] The development of a cohesive national executive branch of government with a chief executive officer for The United Methodist Church may result in an effective structure for the twenty-first century.

CHAPTER 8

Can the Giant Awaken?

And behold, an Ethiopian, a eunuch, a minister of the Candace, queen of the Ethiopians, in charge of all her treasure, had come to Jerusalem to worship and was returning; seated in his chariot, he was reading the prophet Isaiah. And the Spirit said to Philip, "Go up and join this chariot." So Philip ran to him, and heard him reading Isaiah the prophet, and asked, "Do you understand what you are reading?" And he said, "How can I, unless some one guides me?" (Acts 8:27*b*-31*a*)

In August of 1987, the writer (EL) was waiting in the Los Angeles Airport for a flight. Sitting in the adjacent seat was a nice looking man and conversation began with the usual questions: Where are you going? Where do you live? What do you do? When asked my profession, I said, "I am a Bible teacher." The young man cocked his head and replied, "Lady, if I believed half of what you Christians say you believe, I wouldn't sleep tonight. I'd be out telling everybody!" Looking straight into his eyes, I responded, "Thank you for that, I needed it, and I'm going to start with you." I shared with him what God has done and is doing in my life and asked if he didn't want to say yes! to God's love and forgiveness. Without hesitation, he accepted Jesus as Savior and Lord.

Since that holy moment I have thought a great deal about that young man and his readiness to experience God's saving power. I have prayed for him to find the church in which he can experience acceptance, love, nurturing, and challenge, for he is like a newborn baby; care is essential. This young man shares a common need with the Ethiopian eunuch spoken of in the Scripture above. The eunuch needed guidance in understanding the passage he was reading from Isaiah, and he asked for help from Philip. As Philip opened up the Scripture, the eunuch believed and was baptized.

There are thousands of individuals sitting adjacent to us at airports, or seated in chariots along the roadways asking, "How can I know, unless there is someone to guide me?" May we as the Body of Christ hear and respond to this cry!

* * * *

For six years, while serving as Virginia Conference lay leader, Robert B. Carpenter, Jr., published *The Sleeping Giant*, a quarterly newsletter for Virginia Conference laity. The masthead carried the quotation mentioned earlier and attributed to Bishop Nolan B. Harmon: "The laity of the [United] Methodist Church is like unto a 'sleeping giant'—if it is aroused—great things can happen [in the name of Jesus Christ]." This statement occurred while Bishop Harmon was teaching a course based on his 1955 book entitled *Understanding the Methodist Church*. In a similar vein, Janice Grana of *The Upper Room* has quoted Douglas Steere as referring to this lethargy of the church as "sleep walking." It is a form of going through the motion, but at the same time freezing out the deeper walk with Christ. Bishop Richard B. Wilke quotes Robert Schuller who spoke to the 1985 National Congress of United Methodist Men. "He said that very little doubt existed in his mind that The United Methodist Church today is a sleeping giant. Stirred into action, it could produce in our time the most sweeping spiritual, social, economic and political changes in the history of this world."[1] In our introduction we spoke of the church being like Gulliver, bound in his sleep by the "little people." Can the laity awaken? Can the bindings of the "little people" be broken? If so, The United Methodist Church can rise once more to the greatness to which God has called her.

Awaken the Leadership of the Laity

The leadership of the United Methodist laypeople must be awakened. The clergy of our denomination must be prepared to be involved in the development of lay leadership at every level of our connectional system. No longer can our church be a clergy dominated organization. Our laypeople must be accepted by the clergy as full partners in the mission and ministry of The United Methodist Church. In fact, the clergy need the leadership of the laity in order to function at their most effective level of ministry.

The failure of our clergy to fully accept the laypeople can be amply demonstrated by numerous stories from across the church. In one annual conference, when the clergy were in executive session for the report of the Conference Board of Ordained Ministry, it was suggested that the laity might wish to go shopping. In another annual conference, it was suggested that a separate lay session coinciding with the executive session of the clergy was unnecessary except when General and Jurisdictional Conference delegates were being elected. In many respects the sessions of annual conferences give the appearance of being for clergy, by clergy, and of clergy. No where is this more apparent that on the platform of some annual conferences. Instead of seating just the bishop, conference council on ministries director and district superintendents on the platform, full inclusiveness and simple fairness would result in the seating of the conference lay leader and district lay leaders with their clerical counterpart. Such an action would make a major point without a word being spoken. Half of the *members* of each annual conference are lay and half are clergy. Full partnership would require that the annual conference be less of an annual convention of the clergy, and more of an annual meeting of the church.

Bishop Earl G. Hunt, Jr., makes the point clearly in *A Bishop Speaks His Mind* that strong, vigorous lay participation must occur in The United Methodist Church.

> We who are clergy must convince our laypeople that *they are really important to us*, not simply as parishioners to be served, but as counselors to be heard. . . . They must be made aware of our *genuine respect* as well as our *pastoral love.*[2]

All too often laity and clergy do not enter into a relationship conducive to mutual understanding, love, and servant ministry. The fault does not lie solely with either group, but both must share the all-too-common failure to seek out the other in love and acceptance.

Should our denomination move to full partnership between clergy and laity, certain risks will occur. With a less dominant clergy, "more laypersons may actually begin to exercise power. They may make mistakes; they may subscribe to a theology that is perceived to be too conservative or certainly different from what is being taught in the schools of theology. They may challenge and change the accepted ways of doing things; they may even become enthusiastic and excited about their religion."[3] What an amazing possibility—a laity that is so awake, so much a part of The United

Methodist Church that it becomes excited and enthusiastic about its faith! Such a laity would, indeed, awaken the clergy of our denomination and such a partnership would produce wonders for the kingdom of God.

Johnson and Waltz state that "at all levels of the church laypersons as leaders can both stimulate and support the leadership of others."[4] Leadership training has been one of the most amazing aspects of the phenomenal success of the United Methodist Women. This great organization has carefully and productively developed outstanding leadership, not only for the organization of the United Methodist Women, but for the denomination at all levels. One of the most significant failures of United Methodist laity has been in the area of leadership development. The accumulated skill in leadership training of United Methodist laypeople, developed through their workplace and other volunteer organizations, has not been shared within the church in an intentional manner. Particularly in the local church the plaintive cry for trained leadership constantly recurs. The laity of the church, with the pastor, must accept responsibility for training the lay leadership. "The continual search and training for leadership is a primary task of laypersons."[5]

The need for leadership is most dramatically felt in the role of lay leader: local church lay leader, district lay leader, and conference lay leader. These positions are of the utmost importance, and yet all too often they are filled in a perfunctory fashion. These key leaders of the denomination must be selected with care and appropriately trained for the mission and ministry of the church. Bishop Duecker states that although the position of lay leader was established in 1939 for the newly formed Methodist Church, the role was not clear then, nor is it clear now.[6] The 1940 *Doctrines and Discipline of The Methodist Church* contains less than two pages in the local church section dealing with lay activities in charges:

> The Charge Lay Leader of the Station Church shall co-operate with the Pastor in giving full direction to the work of the Official Board, co-operate with the District Lay Leader in the program of Lay Activities for the District, and make a written report to the Quarterly Conference and annually to the District Lay Leader.[7]

In the intervening forty-eight years, not much has changed. The 1988 *Discipline* speaks to the activities of the local church lay leader in as sparse a manner as its predecessors.[8] No where does there seem to be a place for the local church lay leader in the spiritual life of the congregation. Yet this position gives the greatest promise for full partnership with the pastors of The United Methodist Church. Careful selection of the local church lay leader by the nominating committee and appropriate training could produce a valuable asset to The United Methodist Church.

Equally important in the partnership between the clergy and the laity are the positions of district lay leader and conference lay leader. The careful cultivation of individuals for these important jobs can produce persons who have the ability and the capability of providing major leadership to the denomination. In addition, other key leadership resides within the United Methodist Women and United Methodist Men at all levels of the church. These organizations play a major role in the development of lay leadership for the church. With these laypeople working in partnership with the clergy of the denomination, The United Methodist Church can awaken. We need to remember, however, as Wilson has stated that

> Christianity is, after all, too important to be left solely to the clergy. The significant participation of large numbers of laypersons in the operation of the local church and the denomination may be just what is needed to challenge the clergy and to shake the denomination out of its doldrums.[9]

Awaken the Laity Spiritually

For years too many of the laity of The United Methodist Church have been asleep spiritually. For the giant to awaken, the laypeople of the denomination must be awakened spiritually. It would not be inappropriate to include the clergy here as well. For it appears to us that our United Methodist clergy may be just as asleep spiritually as our laity. Laypeople all across the denomination are asking for tools with which to develop their spiritual lives. They recognize that their spiritual lives need exercise just as their physical bodies require it. But the issue always is one of wanting to be spiritually active, but somehow not quite knowing how. A variety of possible mechanisms are available for developing the spiritual lives of laity and clergy alike, including Covenant Discipleship groups and Emmaus communities, among others. However, as a denomination, we have not set out to intentionally develop our spiritual lives. The Upper Room continues to fill the breach, including a congregationally based spiritual development effort following the Lay Spiritual Development program in Virginia.

Although it appears simplistic to state that the laity (and clergy) need to be awakened spiritually, it is only through the development of our spiritual lives that we can truly awaken the giant known as The United Methodist Church. Only by undergirding the denomination with gifts and graces of the Spirit can we be the church God has called us to be. In order to reawaken our nation and our world, we must first awaken ourselves to the power of the Holy Spirit in our lives and in the life of our beloved church.

Awaken the Laity Theologically and Scripturally

In order to be awakened theologically and scripturally, United Methodist laypeople simply must read—read the Scriptures and read the appropriate material needed to understand the Scriptures, both biblically and theologically. Bishop Earl G. Hunt, Jr., makes this point emphatically when he writes, "It is the responsibility of the average layperson in our church to become a *literate Christian.*"[10] All too often, laypeople fail to advance in their theological and biblical knowledge, seeming to rationalize away the need to be literate Christians. If the giant is to awaken, our United Methodist laypeople must once again study the Bible and study theology.

As mentioned earlier, the *Disciple* Bible study program has rapidly developed in popularity. This clearly demonstrates the innate and intense desire of United Methodist laypeople to read and understand the Bible. In format, appeal, and depth, this study has the possibility of reawakening in the average layperson the deep desire to begin a lifelong continuing study of Scripture. With the rapid and early acceptance of this methodology, our denomination must expand on this effort by developing a similar unit of study covering Wesleyan theology. Laypeople and clergy alike need to be grounded in the theology that sets Methodists apart from other Christian denominations across the world. Just as today through the use of the *Disciple* Bible study, United Methodists are being awakened scripturally, so they need to be awakened theologically.

This is particularly vital today as so many individuals are joining United Methodist churches by transfer from other denominations.

In being awakened theologically, we must never forget that United Methodists are Wesleyans first. Our laypeople "should accept the fact that Christianity has two dimensions, *vertical and horizontal.*"[11] Clearly the vertical dimension refers to our relationship with God. The horizontal dimension deals with our relationships within our society. Wesley called us to vital piety that flows naturally into a social righteousness. We cannot be wholly saved until those around us have been saved. United Methodist laity must be awakened theologically in order to be awakened to the needs of those around them. We have been called to spread scriptural holiness across the land. To do so we must clearly understand scripturally and theologically *why* we have been called by God to do so.

Awaken the Laity Evangelically

All Christians have been called to spread the Good News of Jesus Christ across the world. "The Great Commission" (Matt. 28:19-20) demands of all Christians that they become evangels, the bearers of the Good News. Somehow through the years too many United Methodist laity have lost the desire to evangelize the world. Somehow, the term "evangelism" has lost it simple meaning of being about the work of bearing the Good News, and has somehow become fraught with negative connotations. If The United Methodist Church is to grow in the future, the laypeople of the denomination must be awakened to evangelism.

For church growth to occur the clergy must also be awakened. Our seminaries have produced a full generation of United Methodist clergy who have not been grounded in the basic concepts of evangelism. Retraining ordained ministers currently serving must be accomplished in order to equip them to develop and train laypeople for the task of bearing the Good News to those with whom they come in contact. United Methodist schools of theology must develop courses in the Master of Divinity program that will equip seminary students for this role in the future. Conference Boards of Ordained Ministry are in a unique position to assist this effort by requiring all candidates for ordination to take one or two courses in evangelism while in seminary. Clergy well prepared and carefully trained in valid Wesleyan techniques of evangelism are required to awaken United Methodist laity evangelically. Laity awakened to evangelism will have the skills and knowledge necessary to be true evangels, bearers of the Good News of Jesus Christ.

Awaken the Laity to Stewardship

The laity of The United Methodist Church need to be awakened to the requirements of stewardship. Stewardship has had the connotation of tithing, tithing possessions, basically money. As Christians we are called by Jesus in parable after parable to be good stewards. Unfortunately, we usually associate stewardship with what we accomplish with our money. All of us are familiar with the old adage, "Time is money!" Of course it is! In a very real sense as human beings we are endowed with only one true attribute, the lives that we have been given by God. What we United Methodist laity do with the lives we have been given will determine what kind of stewards we really are. We can indeed turn the time that composes our lives into money and then be concerned with the stewardship of our possessions. But over and above such a traditional approach to the stewardship of possessions must be a basic stewardship of our lives.

Therefore, for United Methodist laity to be awakened to stewardship, we must clearly understand that we are called to a stewardship of the gifts and graces with which we have been endowed. In addition we are called to be accountable for the time that God has allotted to us on earth. Robert B. Carpenter, Jr., former Virginia Annual Conference lay leader, refers to the need to be accountable as good stewards for the potential of the power that lies within us. Stewardship cannot mean just being accountable for our possessions, but must mean accountability for all of the life God has given us. United Methodist laypeople must be awakened to this level of accountability for their lives.

Awaken the Laity to Ministry

By their baptism, United Methodist laity are called to the general ministry of the church. In order to awaken the giant, the laypeople of our denomination must be awakened to their call to ministry. Johnson and Waltz, in *Facts and Possibilities*, share the need for laypeople to be involved with "the clear expression of the vision for the congregation [which] will enable persons to contribute their skills and talents to the enhancement of the congregation and the church at large."[12] The ministry of the laity is a clarion call for involvement at all levels of our society and all levels of our denomination.

> Laypersons and ministers alike are willing to commit themselves to needed actions when they clearly understand the vision and have confidence in those who bring the challenge to them. The foremost concern for those in the church must be to share with others God's grace and mercy in the ministries of witness and service. The challenge before the church is to recognize, nurture, and encourage those who can lead in this ministry in Christ's name.[13]

There is a clear need to develop within the laity of The United Methodist Church a feeling of wanting to be deeply involved in the ministry of service and caring.

However, the clergy of our denomination must be willing to empower the laypeople in ministry. Some changes have allowed the laity to be involved in positions of power and decision making. This has helped with the development of lay leadership, but "while The United Methodist Church has provided for more significant involvement of laypersons in the life of the church, it has not developed a modern counterpart to the kind of missional lay involvement typified by the class meeting of an earlier era."[14] United Methodist laity must view themselves as being in mission and ministry to their world. The United Methodist Church cannot be allowed to be so absorbed in local church organization that all the laypeople do is institutional chores. We must release them to be in ministry in the world.[15] If our denomination is not careful, it will continue to encourage laypeople to view the "real Christian" as someone who is involved in the church in a full-time professional ministry. The ministry of service and caring provided by laypeople cannot be viewed as being of a lesser order than that provided by the ordained members of the denomination.[16]

Laypeople are called to be accountable for their ministry as well as to be accountable for how they envision the relationship of their ministry with that of their ordained sisters and brothers. Bishop Hunt strongly reminds the laity that

> The church member should realize always that the concept of the priesthood of all believers makes him or her a minister also, though not ordained, and so causes destructive criticisms of the preacher to be, in the end, a kind of family denial.[17]

A part of the ministry to which laypeople are called is to be in ministry to their pastor. That ministry calls them to support, love, and assistance. As partners who have been awakened to each other, clergy and laity alike will awaken the giant.

Awaken the Laity to Accountability

The laity of The United Methodist Church are called to awaken to the need for accountability. There are two ways in which they are expected to consider this requirement: first, they must be accountable for their own call to discipleship by the Risen Christ; and, second, they must expect and exact accountability on the part of the church itself. Answering the call to discipleship places on the individual the requirement for both types of accountability. For the giant to awaken, laypeople must awaken to the need for accountability in their own lives and in the life of the church.

If United Methodist laity are to be the disciples God has called them to be, they must be willing to hold themselves accountable for their action or inaction. We are called both to serve God and to serve humanity. Failure on our part to accept the servant ministry of all Christians has been a part of the decline of our denomination. If we are serious in our concern about the decline of United Methodism in the United States, then we must stand clearly accountable for our inaction. Our discipleship can and will make the difference. We must be awakened to the need to hold ourselves accountable to God and one another if our discipleship is to make a difference in our lives and in the life of the world.

We are also called as laypeople to hold The United Methodist Church and its agencies accountable. Alan K. Waltz states the situation succinctly when he writes, "The United Methodist laity today is becoming increasingly vocal and assertive in requiring responsive and accountable leadership at all levels of the denomination. Members are eager to know that their expressed concerns are being heard at other levels of the denomination and that the support they give (time, personnel, financial) is being used wisely."[18] Agencies at all levels of the denomination that fail to heed this lay accountability do so at their peril. Such failure to heed this call may, as mentioned by Bishop Hunt, bring us "to a breaking point in our relationship to the *average* [lay] member of The United Methodist Church."[19] United Methodist laity must be awakened to the need to hold the church and its agencies accountable at all levels.

Awaken the Laity to Goodness

In their book *Ministry of the Laity*, James D. Anderson and Ezra Earl Jones assert:

> Real lay ministry, . . . has to do with the character of our lives rather than simply our activity in church. It is a state of heart and mind in which one does the truthful, courageous, and moral thing. Real lay ministry is living responsibly and acting with integrity. It is an outward expression of Christian beliefs.[20]

United Methodist laity must be awakened to goodness, awakened to living out their Christian faith in the world.

What does it mean to be good? Anderson and Jones, referring to the writing of Christopher Alexander, architect and director of the Center for Environmental Structure at the University of California, Berkeley, state that the good is alive; it is whole; it is free. In addition, this quality of being is eternal, "here again the word fails us because the good is so ordinary, so much a part of life."[21] It has always been so. In Genesis (1:31*a*) we read, "God saw all that he had made, and it was very good" (NIV). From the creation of the first layman and the first laywoman, God blessed them and called them good. Indeed they were the very people of God (Laos). "The search which we make for this quality, in our lives, is the central search of any person, and the crux of any individual person's story. It is the search for those moments and situations when we are most alive."[22] United Methodist laity are called to awaken to goodness.

How can laypeople be awakened to "care for our world, ourselves, and our neighbors so that the results are good and so that good can in turn compound the good for all"?[23] In an effort to make this question manageable Anderson and Jones develop the metaphor of a mountain home. In summary, we are asked to imagine that we have retired and purchased a mountain home. We are able to afford this property since its previous owners have allowed it to fall into disrepair as well as stripped it of vegetation, with the resulting erosion and silting of streams. In short, the land has been ruined and the home allowed to disintegrate from abuse and mismanagement. We are asked to consider how we would go about bringing repair and rehabilitation to the home and land.

As in most of life, even if we had the resources, there is no way that all the repairs could be made at once either to the home or to the land. "Hope rests in the direction of patient repair by small increments. And yet each small repair, if it is to be good, cannot be regarded as a solitary act. It must be a part of a process in harmony with the patterns that in concert create a good environment."[24] Slowly but surely, one step at a time, we repair the ravages of the previous owner. So it is as United Methodist laity awaken to goodness in their lives. For it is through the living of good lives that we demonstrate to the world around us that the giant is awakening.

Awakening the laity to goodness (the ministry of the laity)

> is the outward, active, expressive life and activity of people who regard themselves as belonging to the people of God. This ministry is largely carried out in the pluralistic modern world, which is a non-Christian context. It is a world that can be, and is even now being, transformed and repaired by God.[25]

It is through a laity awakened to goodness that the power of God's love is brought to a hurting world.

Conclusion

The giant can awaken! But the giant can awaken and cast off the bonds of the "little" people only as the laity of The United Methodist Church awaken. They must be awakened spiritually, theologically, scripturally, and evangelically to leadership, stewardship, ministry, accountability, and goodness. Only as the laypeople awaken will our denomination awake and become the church God created her to be. Bishop Richard Wilke quotes Robert Schuller, speaking to the 1985 National Congress of United Methodist Men:

> The United Methodist Church has the theology and the organization to literally sweep this country for Jesus Christ. No other denomination has the power, the ability or the freedom to attract the masses of people as does The United Methodist Church; this giant has been lulled to sleep. If this church begins to flaunt what it has and this giant begins to wake up, watch out, for it could literally change the world for Christ.[26]

An awakened laity and an awakened United Methodist Church can and will change the world!

CHAPTER 9

A Lay Prescription for The United Methodist Church?

As we come to the conclusion of this book, our intention is to explicitly set forth our prescriptions for The United Methodist Church. We do not expect that everyone will agree with them, nor do we expect that all of them will be accepted. We are, however, giving to our church for her consideration our prayerful and thoughtful suggestions, which we believe will awaken the slumbering and bound giant that we know as The United Methodist Church. We believe the time is now for this giant to test the ropes that bind it, in order that it might fulfill its great potential of service and witness to God.

We have called our suggestions "prescriptions." Just as a physician writes a separate and individual prescription for each remedy for a patient, so we are writing separate and individual remedies for the maladies that we perceive within The United Methodist Church. Each prescription, if accepted and used, should have an impact on successfully treating the sleeping giant. We sincerely hope that our prescriptions are viewed as our best effort to cure our patient.

The Prescriptions

℞ 1   The United Methodist Church must proclaim and embody the stewardship of all of life.

Too often for United Methodists stewardship simply means tithing or financial campaigns or giving money. For too long we have been known as a people who will pass a collection plate anytime, anywhere. Indeed we need to be about the stewardship of our possessions, but God expects more of United Methodists than simply giving money. God expects of us a stewardship of all of life, of the very life that he has given to each one of us as individuals, and the life of our denomination that he has given to us corporately. Our church must be intentional about its efforts to proclaim the stewardship of all of life; time, talents, and possessions. Until we embody such a form of stewardship in our individual lives and in the corporate life of our denomination, we will be unable to face a hurting, weary world. We believe that The United Methodist Church has been called by God to proclaim such a stewardship.

℞ 2   The United Methodist Church should empower and train laypeople to be in servant ministry to their communities.

The laypeople of The United Methodist Church must be trained in order to serve in ministry to one another and the people of their communities. The clergy of the denomination are logical trainers of the laity, but to effectively perform this task, clergy must be prepared to empower laypeople to serve effectively. The laity in this instance must be viewed as Christians serving the Risen Lord in partnership with those ordained to ministry. Such a partnership in ministry of clergy and laity will produce an effect that cannot be calculated. Laypeople must recognize that ordination is not required to be in effective ministry to their community. Gus Gustafson in *"I Was . . . Called to Be a Layman"*[1] clearly points the way to servant ministry of laypeople. The laity of The United Methodist Church have been called to be in ministry just as the clergy have been called to serve God and humankind by being set apart. We believe that an empowered and trained laity can serve in partnership with the clergy in a manner that will tremendously enhance the servant ministry of The United Methodist Church.

℞ 3   The United Methodist Church must awaken within both laypeople and clergy the knowledge of the sacred worth of each human life, and seek to bring reconciliation, renewal, healing, and hope to everyone.

It is too easy for each of us to fail daily in our efforts to recognize the sacred worth of all members of humanity. We must be about the business as a denomination of assisting our people never to forget that it is God who has made each one of us, and therefore we are all good. We recall the punch line of a famous story that ends, "God didn't make no junk!" We are precious in his sight and we are called to hold each person precious in our own sight. We have been sent to seek and to save the lost, to bring the message of reconciliation to a warring world, to renew a tired old world in the love of Jesus Christ, to bring healing to a world that hurts, and to proclaim Christian hope to a hopeless day. We believe that God has called the two of us, as well each of you, to this day, to this place in which we live and work, to this world for such a servant ministry.

℞ 4 The United Methodist Church must provide opportunities for meaningful Bible study made available to and promoted by the local church.

For too long The United Methodist Church has failed to emphasize in-depth Bible study. Too many United Methodists are biblically illiterate, a situation that must be remedied as soon as possible. Clearly the *Disciple* Bible study can make a major difference in the life of the denomination and the local congregations. But we must remember that when disciple groups have completed this effort, there will be a need for follow-up material that will provide for the in-depth study of Scripture. Our efforts in this arena as a denomination must be of a continuing nature. Rapid, but careful, planning must be carried out as soon as possible in order that the necessary material is developed and available as needed. We believe that United Methodists must be a people of "one book" and therefore biblically literate.

℞ 5 Christian spiritual formation, being formed into the fullness of Christ, must become the major goal of United Methodist Christian education and ministry.

Life, by its very nature, is spiritual formation. The question then becomes, In what kind of spiritual formation are we engaged? Out of the deep hunger of laity and clergy alike to be involved in deepening and strengthening their spiritual nature, The United Methodist Church must address the spiritual life of both the local congregation and each individual church member. Some of the United Methodist books, periodicals, and church school materials are leading the way in Christian spiritual formation. However, local churches need to take advantage of such literature and encourage the forming of groups, classes and/or retreats for the spiritual inward journey. We believe that the key function of our Christian education and ministry must be to develop disciples grounded in a personal and corporate spirituality.

℞ 6   Within The United Methodist Church, full partnership between laity and clergy must be affirmed, represented, and accepted at every level of our connectional system.

The time has come and passed when the laity of The United Methodist Church will accept anything less than a full partnership with the ordained ministers of our church. Likewise, the clergy should expect, if not demand, such a level of commitment on the part of their parishioners. All members of The United Methodist Church have been called to servant ministry, therefore there must be a close partnership in the process of being evangels, the bearers of the Good News. For it is as evangelists that all of us have been called by the words of Jesus in the Great Commission. The task of making disciples and remaking old ones is too important to leave in the hands of just the clergy, or just the laity. It is of such utmost importance that it can only be accomplished by every one of us working together in partnership. A clericalized denomination has outlived its usefulness. We believe that God has called us as a denomination to be in servant ministry to the world for it is the parish of all of us, laity and clergy alike.

℞ 7   The United Methodist Church should expect pastors to view their servant ministry as a calling of God, not as a profession.

Too much emphasis has been placed on the professionalization of the ordained ministry of The United Methodist Church. Our pastors, we believe, have been called by God to a servant ministry to the people of God (Laos). That they have standing as a professional individual is secondary to this calling. This is a particularly important aspect of the United Methodist clergy since our system is one of being sent (appointed) to a local congregation. Our local congregations are dependent, therefore, on having sent to them pastors who are seen by their peers as having been called by

God to ministry, rather than viewing themselves as professional ministers. The laity of The United Methodist Church indeed do want it both ways. We want highly educated and skilled professionals as our pastors, but we want this attribute to be secondary to their being called by God to servant ministry. As a result, we believe that Boards of Ordained Ministry—indeed, all levels that examine candidates—must carefully screen individuals who desire ordination in The United Methodist Church, in order to clearly determine the driving force in the lives of candidates for ordination.

℞ 8   The United Methodist Church should use the number of confessions of faith as the church growth barometer when evaluating the effectiveness of ordained ministers.

Transfer of membership from one local church to another regardless of denomination simply relocates individuals already a part of the Body of Christ. Only individuals coming into that Body through the means of professing their faith are really new members of the church. As long as The United Methodist Church relies on simply transferring membership between churches, the denomination will not grow, nor will the Church, the Body of Christ, grow. Unless Committees on Pastor-Parish Relations use the number of new Christians brought into the fellowship of the church as a major parameter for evaluating the servant ministry of the clergy, there will not be a major emphasis on expanding the Church universal by winning new people to Christ.

As a denomination, The United Methodist Church has failed in recent years to place emphasis on conversion as the major route for bringing new disciples into a relationship with the church. All of us place our emphasis in life on those things with which we are evaluated. We do not expect that our United Methodist clergy will be vastly different from the society within which they live and work. Therefore, we believe that each United Methodist pastor must be evaluated on the effectiveness of his or her ministry to the unchurched. This can only be effectively done by considering the number of individuals brought into relationship with The United Methodist Church by confession of faith.

℞ 9   The United Methodist Church should appoint pastors based
on their gifts and graces and the needs of the local
congregations; not on seniority and/or salary.

The seniority system for the appointment of United Methodist
clergy simply does not address the needs of the denomination for
the deployment of its clergy. It results in individuals who "flop to
the top."[2] Our local churches deserve better. Until bishops and
their cabinets are willing to appoint United Methodist clergy on the
basis of the needs of the local church, our denomination will
continue to have difficulty matching pastors with the requisite skills
with the local congregations that have a need for those skills.
Conference needs, and the needs of the clergy, must be secondary
to the needs of the local church. A consequence of failing to do so
will result in local congregations lowering the salary level in an
effort to reset their position in the seniority system of the annual
conference. This will result in the unfortunate situation of a
decrease in the average salary paid to United Methodist clergy. We
believe that United Methodist laity will be willing to set appropriate
salaries for their pastors, particularly when they find that they have
been provided a pastor based on their needs and the pastor's skills.

℞ 10   The United Methodist Church should emphasize providing
leadership for the ministry needs of the congregation, not
the personal, financial, or professional needs of the ordained
minister.

Such a statement appears harsh on its surface. But if United
Methodist clergy enter the servant ministry of the church based on a
call by God, then their personal and family needs will no longer be
paramount. This does not mean that such needs should never be
considered, but United Methodist ministers enter our connectional
system understanding that they will be deployed to the local
congregations by being sent to them, not by being called by the
congregation. If the bishops and cabinets consider the needs of the
congregations, rather than the needs of the clergy, well-matched
appointments will be made. All too often it is the needs of the
pastors that result in their staying beyond the point of being the
most effective. Likewise, the needs of annual conferences may

result in pastors being moved before they have had the opportunity to reach their most effective ministry to a local congregation. Working spouses and clergy couples further complicate the matter. We believe that the appropriate provision for the leadership needs of the local congregation will provide the best deployment of pastors within The United Methodist Church.

℞ 11   The United Methodist Church should abolish the guaranteed appointment system for ordained ministers.

The guaranteed appointment system for United Methodist pastors is in many aspects the root of many of the problems related to United Methodist clergy. If there were no guaranteed appointment system, many of the questions concerning competency of ordained ministers would be answered. If ministers in full connection were not guaranteed appointments, incompetent pastors would not need to be appointed. There appears to be no rationale at this point in the history of The United Methodist Church to continue the system that provides employment for United Methodist pastors irrespective of ability, competence, or diligence to their calling. This is particularly true with an appointment system that rewards seniority and not ability. We believe that the guaranteed appointment system has outlived its usefulness and should be abolished.

℞ 12   The United Methodist Church should develop a method for evaluation of the clergy resulting in incompetence being treated as a performance, not a disciplinary, problem.

United Methodist laity deserve competent clergy. A high percentage of our pastors are competent and diligent. However, the small number of incompetent pastors are a major problem at the local church level, as well as at the annual conference level. Currently the issue concerning competency of United Methodist clergy is treated in the same manner that issues of moral turpitude are treated. Every annual conference must be able to assist incompetent clergy gracefully to leave The United Methodist Church. Instead, such individuals are too often sent year after year to serve another unfortunate United Methodist congregation. In the course of their career, it is difficult to determine how many local congregations are blighted by such incompetence.

An effective system of evaluation must be developed so that incompetent clergy can be clearly identified, and a system of dealing with issues of performance must be developed that will allow pastors who consistently fail to meet the minimum standards of performance to leave the denomination gracefully. Such an effort will require that we assist such individuals in retraining in order that they will be able to leave the ordained ministry having been dealt with compassionately. For The United Methodist Church to do otherwise will simply continue to unfairly treat both the incompetent pastor and the local church to which such a pastor is appointed.

℞ 13   The United Methodist Church should require a responsible level of pastoral accountability.

Unless district superintendents work more closely with local church Committees on Pastor-Parish Relations, the clergy of The United Methodist Church will continue to be ineffectively supervised. Many United Methodist clergy are self-starters and require little supervision, but when this is not the case, the current system of evaluation and supervision is ineffective. District superintendents may be elders just as the ministers assigned to the churches on their district, but they have been appointed to serve as presiding elders. This position requires that they be willing to exert a responsible degree of supervision insofar as the pastors assigned to their district are concerned. This means that when they determine in association with a local church Committee on Pastor-Parish Relations that a problem in pastoral leadership is present, they perform the superintending function. United Methodist pastors must be accountable for their time, effort, energy, not only to God, but to their district superintendent and Committee on Pastor-Parish Relations.

℞ 14   The United Methodist Church should require the pastor to be the chief Christian educator of the local congregation.

If The United Methodist Church is to grow and to educate the laity of the denomination, the pastor must be the chief Christian educator of the local church. This clearly requires the pastor not only to assist in the development of the program of Christian education within the local congregation, but to teach as well. The development of the *Disciple* Bible study has significantly enhanced this possibility since it requires the minister to be involved with the teaching function. Many United Methodist pastors believe that they must be a part of this program to be seen as supporting a denominational effort. Many more want to be a part of the *Disciple* program because they believe that such an effort of combining Bible study and discipleship is long overdue. For whatever reason, many United Methodist pastors are participating in this major effort. By so doing they are involving themselves in the process of being the chief Christian educator of their local congregation. This will assist in providing the needed emphasis on the process of Christian education in the local church.

℞ 15 The United Methodist Church should require training in evangelism for all seminary students and continuing education courses in evangelism for all clergy serving the local church.

For too long, we have left the curriculum of United Methodist seminary students up to the faculty of the schools of theology. It is clearly a process that is too important to so do. In order to determine the training of seminary students, annual conference Boards of Ordained Ministry should establish required courses for admission to full connection. Courses in evangelism must be required of all United Methodist seminary students. At least one such course should be designed with practical applications. If we are called as Christians to make disciples, then our clergy must be well-grounded in the theory and practice of doing so. Only with such a background can they enable and train the laity of the local church to be about the task of making disciples.

Since many United Methodist ministers have not been trained in evangelism during their seminary education, all United Methodist pastors serving in local churches must be required to participate in continuing education programs designed to provide these skills. We recognize that we can require people to participate in continuing education, but cannot force them to learn what is being taught. Nonetheless, perhaps there will be a heightened awareness on the part of the laity of the local church that evangelism is a major area of emphasis within our denomination. Their interest may spark the interest of their pastor, resulting in a marked improvement in the effectiveness of denominational evangelistic efforts.

℞ 16   The United Methodist Church should reestablish a strong system of part-time lay pastors and local preachers.

Methodism in its early days relied almost exclusively on lay pastors and local preachers. During the period of the recurring mergers leading to The United Methodist Church, the use of lay pastors and local preachers, particularly on a part-time basis, declined rather dramatically in most parts of the United States. The small, usually rural, United Methodist churches hunger for a pastor who stays with them longer than is usual with either a student pastor or a minister appointed to serve a multi-church charge. Increasing the use of lay pastors and local preachers, particularly on a part-time basis, provides the opportunity for small churches to be served by individuals who will live in the community for a longer period of time. This will provide for a significant ministry for laypeople, while at the same time meeting the needs of smaller churches. Needless to say, such individuals should be assigned to a supervising minister in full connection in the particular annual conference.

℞ 17   The United Methodist Church, in order to recapture her traditional Wesleyan emphasis on evangelism and education, should divide the General Board of Discipleship, deliberately re-creating the General Board of Evangelism and the General Board of Education.

The organizational structure created in 1972 has resulted in the two areas, evangelism and education, becoming lost in the bureaucracy of the General Board of Discipleship. This organizational structure appeared to have significant possibility for the future, but it is apparent that it has not fulfilled its high expectations, particularly in these two major areas. As sections of a division of the General Board of Discipleship, these key areas have been unable to compete adequately with other major areas of the general church structure. Thus their funding levels have decreased, and they are no longer major forces in the life of the denomination. As a result, the activities of local churches and annual conferences have markedly diminished in these areas to the detriment of The United Methodist Church.

In order to once again establish evangelism and education as major forces within our denomination, we believe that The United Methodist Church must deliberately re-create the General Board of Evangelism and the General Board of Education. Only in this way will these two areas be able to compete for funds at the general level and at the same time develop the network of individuals needed to maintain a major thrust across the connection. The development of general boards in these areas will send a message once again to United Methodists that evangelism and education are key areas in the life of our denomination.

₨ 18   The United Methodist Church should emphasize establishing new congregations and revitalizing existing churches as the major means of evangelism, outreach to the unchurched, and church growth.

The United Methodist Church grew when it deliberately planted new churches across the United States. Likewise, the denomination declined in membership when it failed to do so. We have always been a frontier denomination. Throughout our history we have gone where the people are. But in recent years we have simply declined in building new churches. We have built Korean churches, and Hispanic and other Asian churches are developing in major cities; but other denominations have pressed forward more boldly. As a result, we can no longer claim to be the most ethnically diverse denomination in the United States.

Building new churches where the people are means that we must deliberately set about planting new congregations in the growing suburbs of the United States; in areas of urban blight where ethnically centered churches are desperately needed, on the reservations of Native Americans, and in the major ports of entry for new immigrants to this nation. Unless we are willing to raise the money and do the work required to plant new congregations across the United States, as a denomination we can expect to continue to decline, not only numerically, but as a moral and religious force in our nation. We believe that forming new congregations and revitalizing older congregations, particularly in areas of growth within the United States, will allow The United Methodist Church to reach the unchurched millions in the United States.

℞ 19 The United Methodist Church should regain an understanding of Wesleyan theology including the doctrine of original sin, justification by faith, the meaning of grace, the doctrine of Christian perfection, and salvation by faith under the guidance of the Holy Spirit.

To be The United Methodist Church means to be Wesleyan Christian. Our theology cannot be based on personal whim. There *is* a core belief that United Methodists believe. Without such a core we simply blow with the winds of the newest and most popular theology. We are a denomination with a pluralism of people, but not a pluralism of theology. It is difficult enough to train our laypeople in theology; we should not have to train them in multiple theologies, asking them to differentiate between them. We believe that The United Methodist Church must be a denomination grounded in Wesleyan theology and that the laity and clergy alike must recapture this unique Christian perspective.

℞ 20 The United Methodist Church should make the Sunday worship hour a vital experience in the life of the local congregation.

Too often the most boring hour of the week occurs at eleven o'clock on Sunday morning in United Methodist churches across the United States. This need not, and should not, be. Instead this hour of the week should be the most dynamic, exciting, and vital hour of the week. As our people gather to worship, they can, and should, expect United Methodist clergy and laity to lead a vital worship experience. They deserve no less. Great preaching is one thing, vital worship is another. Preaching obviously can assist in developing a vital worship experience, but a vital worship experience can occur without great preaching. The time of worship should assist individuals to encounter the living God. In such a union, lives are transformed, issues of life are addressed, and the Holy Spirit is experienced as Power adequate for the coming week. Not every United Methodist pastor will be a great preacher, but every United Methodist pastor can lead a vital worship experience for the local congregation.

℞ 21   The United Methodist Church should ensure that at all levels of the connectional system the local congregation is the center of the denomination.

The local congregation simply *must* be the center of The United Methodist Church. All levels of the connectional system must ensure that the constant focus of attention is the local church. To fail to do so is to lose sight of the reason for being a connectional system. If the focus is elsewhere, there is no need for a local church to be a part of a connectional system. The local church does not exist for the purpose of providing a support system for the various levels of our denomination. Instead, the rest of the connection exists solely to support the local congregation, working to provide it with the tools to be in ministry in its community. In recent years there has been a significant tendency within the denomination to turn away from the local church focus. We believe that we must reassert the significance of the local church in the life of The United Methodist Church.

℞ 22   All programs of The United Methodist Church should serve the needs and concerns of the local congregation.

Too often the programs at the general church level as well as at the annual conference level are directed to purposes other than serving the needs and concerns of the local church. If The United Methodist Church reasserts the priority of the local church, then the programs designed at all levels will serve the needs of the local church as well as their concern for national and global missions. Programs that do not serve the needs of the local congregation are clearly directed toward other purposes. But the local church is the organization that is asked to provide the funds, personnel, and energy to support programs that are not essential to its life and ministry. We believe that agencies at all levels of the denomination must no longer budget for, or request, programs that do not serve the needs or concerns of the local congregation. We do not believe that local churches should be asked to accept apportionments that fund causes deemed to be inimical to the best interests of the local church and its members.

℞ 23 The United Methodist Church should build or develop a headquarters to serve as a unifying influence on the denomination.

The United Methodist Church stands at a crossroad in its history as it attempts to overcome the vagaries of its various unions. The geographic jurisdictional system has served the denomination well and can continue to do so in the future. However, in an effort to bring full union to The United Methodist Church, it is time that the denomination develop a headquarters. This would serve as a rallying point for the church. It would provide the physical structure that would allow the denomination to cohesively enter the future. It would reduce the fiefdoms of jurisdictional control of staff members of the general agencies. It would provide a United Methodist Center to which the local congregations could turn for assistance. It could provide economies of scale financially by reducing the number of facilities that must be owned or rented. A by-product of such a central structure would be disassociation of general agencies physically from the various interlocking non-United Methodist agencies with which they coexist. A final positive effect would be to allow both lay and clerical staff members to build a career within the denominational structures without having to physically move from one location to another. This would assist in the issue of staff accountability since long tenures in particular positions would no longer be a necessity. Since a feasibility study for the move of the General Board of Global Ministries has been approved by the 1988 General Conference, should such a move be found feasible, the beginning of a United Methodist Center could be established by the careful relocation of this board.

℞ 24 The United Methodist Church should amend its Constitution to establish an executive branch to carry out the mandates of the quadrennial General Conference.

The United Methodist Church has both a legislative branch and a judicial branch within the current structure. However, there is no executive branch with a resulting void in expression of the activity of the denomination. The various general agencies serve many of the functions of an executive branch, except that they have little or no cohesiveness. Each agency tends to act autonomously, on occasions refusing to consider the actions of the legislative branch, the General Conference. In order to develop a cohesive interaction of the various agencies, a formal change to the structure of the church must be made in order to bring together the executive functions. This, of course, could be more readily accomplished by the development of one denominational center. With all the general agencies present in one location, an appropriate denominational executive branch could be developed. We believe that an executive branch would markedly enhance the function of The United Methodist Church, allowing it to more appropriately serve the local church.

℞ 25 The United Methodist Church should amend its Constitution to establish a chief executive officer to be elected from the active members of the Council of Bishops, such an individual having residential and presidential responsibilities for the entire church.

One of the glaring deficiencies of The United Methodist Church is the lack of a chief executive officer. Without a CEO, there is little need for a denominational headquarters and an executive branch. To have all three would effectively bring a quality of accountability to the general level of the church, which is currently non-existent. The CEO position could be established in a variety of ways, but it must as a minimum have authority to deal effectively with the general agencies with veto authority over their actions between quadrennial General Conferences. Clearly, as the sign on President Harry Truman's desk read, "The Buck Stops Here," a CEO would provide the church with the necessary voice to speak authoritatively within the mandates of the General Conference. Until such time as the church creates a position of chief executive officer, the general agencies will continue to pursue their own agendas, often with little regard for the actions of the General Conference or the needs and concerns of the local congregations. We believe that the position of a chief executive officer could best be filled at this time by an active bishop who would serve the entire church instead of an area. The Council of Bishops would provide additional assistance by acting as the board of directors to the CEO. In time, further change could allow for the CEO to be any United Methodist, lay or clergy.

R 26 The United Methodist Church should abolish all quota systems based on race, ethnicity, age, gender, and handicapping condition and the nomination and election of individuals to all positions throughout the denomination should be based on ability.

The United Methodist Church has been exceptionally concerned through the past several decades that all individuals in the denomination be granted full and equal partnership in the affairs of the church. As a result, in an effort to develop full participation, quotas have been established to ensure representation of all individuals based on race, ethnicity, age, gender, and handicapping condition. However, in the effort to be inclusive, the denomination has been unfair to certain other categories of individuals. The abolition of quota systems for filling positions at all levels of the connectional system is a case of simple fairness.

The members of the denomination are sensitive to the needs of all individuals to be included in the life and structures of the church. But to exclude some in order to include others simply produces a system that is no more fair than the system it has replaced. Most, if not all, individuals elected to positions of influence within our church are fully qualified. This being so, why is a quota system necessary? Would it not be far better to elect individuals solely on the principle of ability? We believe that individuals should fill the offices and positions of The United Methodist Church at all levels solely on the basis of ability.

℞ 27 The United Methodist Church should require that all general agencies of the denomination be accountable as the servants of the local church, not as autonomous entities.

All too often the general boards and agencies of the denomination appear to function completely autonomously from the local churches. As a consequence, these agencies are irrelevant to the life of local congregations. The general boards and agencies of The United Methodist church were created to serve the church, particularly the local church, not to serve themselves. Regardless of the facts in the situation, the perception of many laypeople is that these agencies exist to serve themselves, their staff members, and/or their board members. Certainly there are agencies that do serve the local church and there are staff members who are intent in seeing that their agencies do so, but there are likewise agencies that appear not to care about or for their constituency. We believe that the General Conference and the elected members of the boards of these agencies must hold the general boards and agencies accountable; not only accountable for their actions, but accountable to serving the local church. If persons connected with the general agencies cannot or will not serve the local church, we believe that they should be replaced by ones who will.

℞ 28 The United Methodist Church should continue its strong ecumenical dialogue, but should not as a matter of policy consider additional organic mergers in the future.

There is no evidence today that the merging of various denominations strengthens the resulting new organization. In fact, although anecdotal, evidence is accumulating that such mergers result in a weakening of the new church, due to energy being sapped by the merger process. Less than twenty years after the union of The Methodist Church and the Evangelical United Brethren Church, the membership of The United Methodist Church has dropped to a point that simply reflects the loss of the entire EUB denomination. The strength of The United Methodist Church will improve through a variety of other remedies, and at the same time another denomination will not be lost.

Irrespective of merger with other denominations, The United

Methodist Church must continue its strong emphasis on cooperating with other denominations, national, and international organizations and on dialogues of an ecumenical nature. Being unwilling to be a part of mergers as a matter of denominational policy does not indicate a lack of interest in *full* involvement in ecumenical dialogues, particularly through the World Methodist Council and the Consultation on Church Union. Organic union is one thing, ecumenical dialogue and denominational cooperation are another. We give strong support to the latter, while having clear reservations concerning the former.

Is There Hope for Our Church?

We can, without any hesitation, answer the question with a resounding *yes!* There is hope for The United Methodist Church as a denomination; there is hope for United Methodist clergy; there is hope for United Methodist laity! For the United Methodist giant is sleeping, not due to one group, board, agency, or council, but because *all* of us have been asleep. We believe the giant will awaken as we respond to the call to a new life of servant ministry to God's world.

God has called us to this time, place, and church for a purpose. That purpose is for The United Methodist Church to become once again the great moral and religious force that God called her to be. With all United Methodists, laity and clergy alike, awakening to the task God has set before us, we can indeed awaken the giant.

Think with us for a moment of all the churches in your city, town, or countryside. In your mind's eye, place them side by side. Remove all the side walls so that people can move about freely, respectfully, and lovingly among all the churches. There are no barriers. Walk outside and look at this superstructure. There are belfries of all sizes and shapes; there are crosses of different materials and types; no two roof lines are the same; but we have a single church structure. This is the true church; it is the Body of Christ. Christ is the head and the churches are parts of his body, serving in his place. This structure is unique since the individual shape and contour of each church is present within the whole. As we awaken the giant called The United Methodist Church, we hope and pray that each of us may become a part of the whole, while retaining the individual characteristics that make us unique.

What can we expect of a denomination that is filled with awakened United Methodists serving in their local congregations and communities? How do we perceive them as part of The United Methodist Church? A story is told of an American soldier who was killed while serving in France during World War II. His friends wanted to bury him. When they saw a small cemetery near a little church, they wished to bury him there. They approached the pastor of the church and requested permission to bury their comrade. They were quietly told that only church members were allowed to be buried in the little cemetery. Bowing to the rules that forbade them to bury their friend in the cemetery, they dug his grave just outside the cemetery fence. Caught by nightfall, they bivouacked near the French village that night. Early the next morning as they were preparing to depart, they went one last time to visit the grave of their comrade, only to find that during the night the caretaker had moved the fence in order to include the new grave within the little cemetery. Our hope is based on a United Methodist Church that moves fences, because the world is our parish!

NOTES

Chapter 1 Where Are We Today?

1. Douglas F. Cannon, "United Methodist Membership Drops by 70,000," *The United Methodist Reporter*, July 15, 1988, p. 3.
2. Warren J. Hartman, *Membership Trends* (Nashville: Discipleship Resources, 1976), p. 10.
3. Douglas W. Johnson and Alan K. Waltz, *Facts and Possibilities* (Nashville: Abingdon Press, 1987), p. 19.
4. Hartman, *Membership Trends*, pp. 29-33.
5. Ibid., p. 33.
6. Warren J. Hartman, "Our Missing Generation," *Discipleship Trends*, 5:4, 1987, p. 1.
7. Ibid., p. 2.
8. Johnson and Waltz, *Facts and Possibilities*, p. 23.
9. Douglas W. Johnson, *A Study of Data from Former Evangelical United Brethren Churches 1968–1985* (New York: General Board of Global Ministries, The United Methodist Church, 1987), p. 3.
10. Ibid., p. 13.
11. Lyle E. Schaller, *It's a Different World!* (Nashville: Abingdon Press, 1987), p. 77.
12. W. James Cowell, "Denominational Decline and Congregational Development," *New Congregational Development*, a newsletter (Nashville: General Board of Discipleship, The United Methodist Church, n.d.), p. 1.
13. Richard B. Wilke, *And Are We Yet Alive?* (Nashville: Abingdon Press, 1986), p. 25.
14. Johnson and Waltz, *Facts and Possibilities*, p. 41.
15. Halford E. Luccock and Paul Hutchinson, *The Story of Methodism* (Cincinnati: The Methodist Book Concern, 1926), p. 447.
16. Hartman, *Membership Trends*, p. 22.
17. From "Mission Evangelism: New Initiatives for a New Era," in *Mission Papers* (New York: General Board of Global Ministries, The United Methodist Church, 1987), p. 3.
18. "Mission 2000: The Key to Vital Congregations," in *Mission Papers* (New York: General Board of Global Ministries, The United Methodist Church, 1988).
19. Hartman, *Membership Trends*, p. 25.
20. Ibid., p. 13.
21. Ibid., p. 28.

Chapter 2   A Kept Clergy?

1. Dennis M. Campbell, *The Yoke of Obedience* (Nashville: Abingdon Press, 1988), p. 20.
2. Ibid., p. 28.
3. Robert L. Wilson and Steve Harper, *Faith and Form* (Grand Rapids, Mich.: Francis Asbury Press, 1988), p. 89.
4. Ira Gallaway, *Drifted Astray* (Nashville: Abingdon Press, 1983), p. 133.
5. R. Sheldon Duecker, *Tensions in the Connection* (Nashville: Abingdon Press, 1983), p. 37.
6. Ibid., p. 29.
7. *The Book of Discipline of The United Methodist Church, 1988* (Nashville: The United Methodist Publishing House, 1988), par. 531.
8. Duecker, *Tensions in the Connection*, p. 40.
9. *The Book of Discipline*, par. 422.
10. Douglas W. Johnson and Alan K. Waltz, *Facts and Possibilities* (Nashville: Abingdon Press, 1987), p. 80.
11. William H. Willimon and Robert L. Wilson, *Rekindling the Flame* (Nashville: Abingdon Press, 1987), pp. 49-50.
12. Johnson and Waltz, *Facts and Possibilities*, p. 146.
13. Richard B. Wilke, *And Are We Yet Alive?* (Nashville: Abingdon Press, 1986), pp. 102-3.
14. *The Book of Discipline*, par. 436.
15. Ibid., par. 423.
16. Wilke, *And Are We Yet Alive?* p. 101.
17. Duecker, *Tensions in the Connection*, p. 37.
18. *The Book of Discipline*, par. 435.
19. Willimon and Wilson, *Rekindling the Flame*, p. 82.
20. Willimon and Wilson, *Rekindling the Flame,* p. 55.
21. Duecker, *Tensions in the Connection*, p. 38.

Chapter 3   Is the General Church Irrelevant?

1. Earl G. Hunt, Jr., *A Bishop Speaks His Mind* (Nashville: Abingdon Press, 1987), p. 138.
2. *The Book of Discipline of The United Methodist Church, 1988* (Nashville: The United Methodist Publishing House, 1988), par. 15.
3. Ibid., p. 301.

4. R. Sheldon Duecker, *Tensions in the Connection* (Nashville: Abingdon Press, 1983), p. 67.
5. Ibid., p. 67-68.
6. *Daily Christian Advocate*, May 5, 1988, p. 498.
7. Duecker, *Tensions in the Connection*, p. 68.
8. *Advance Edition of the Daily Christian Advocate*, p. H-1-29.
9. Ibid., pp. H-1-30, 31.
10. *Daily Christian Advocate*, May 3, 1988, p. 295.
11. Ibid., p. 644.
12. Duecker, *Tensions in the Connection*, p. 68.
13. Douglas W. Johnson and Alan K. Waltz, *Facts and Possibilities* (Nashville: Abingdon Press, 1987), p. 118.
14. Duecker, *Tensions in the Connection*, p. 88.
15. *The Book of Discipline*, par. 805.1*b*.
16. Ibid., par. 805.2*a*.
17. Johnson and Waltz, *Facts and Possibilities*, p. 53.
18. Ibid.
19. Hunt, *A Bishop Speaks His Mind*, p. 141.
20. Ibid.
21. Ibid.
22. Ibid.
23. *Daily Christian Advocate*, pp. 659-62.
24. Robert L. Wilson and Steve Harper, *Faith and Form* (Grand Rapids, Mich.: Francis Asbury Press, 1988), p. 154.
25. *Daily Christian Advocate*, pp. 684-86.
26. William H. Willimon and Robert L. Wilson, *Rekindling the Flame* (Nashville: Abingdon Press, 1987), p. 95.
27. Duecker, *Tensions in the Connection*, p. 86.
28. Johnson and Waltz, *Facts and Possibilities,* p. 58.
29. Wilson and Harper, *Faith and Form*, p. 43.
30. Duecker, *Tensions in the Connection*, p. 78.
31. Wilson and Harper, *Faith and Form*, p. 161.
32. Willimon and Wilson, *Rekindling the Flame*, pp. 94-95.
33. *The United Methodist Newscope*, 5, March 25, 1977, p. 1.

Chapter 4   What Theology?

1. Nathaniel Hawthorne, *The Complete Short Stories of Nathaniel Hawthorne* (Garden City, N. Y.: Doubleday, 1959), p. 473.
2. *The Book of Discipline, 1988*, p. 78.
3. James W. Fowler, *Stages of Faith* (New York: Harper & Row, 1981), p. 10.

4. "Grace upon Grace," *Advance Edition of the Daily Christian Advocate,* p. C-15.
5. Emerson Colaw, *Beliefs of a United Methodist Christian* (Nashville: Tidings, 1972), p. 25.
6. George Morris, *The Mystery and Meaning of Conversion* (Nashville: Discipleship Resources, 1981), p. 35.
7. *The Book of Discipline of The United Methodist Church, 1984* (Nashville: The United Methodist Publishing House, 1984), p. 76.
8. Mack B. Stokes, *The Holy Spirit in the Wesleyan Heritage* (Nashville: Graded Press/Abingdon Press, 1985), p. 46.
9. E. Stanley Jones, *Conversion* (Nashville: Abingdon Press, 1959), pp. 131-32.
10. John Wesley, *Works*, vol. VI, pp. 74-75.
11. Fowler, *Stages of Faith*, p. 203.
12. Albert C. Outler, *Theology in the Wesleyan Spirit* (Nashville: Tidings, 1975), p. 9.
13. Ibid., p. 13.
14. Ibid., p. 6.
15. *The Book of Discipline, 1988,*p. 81.
16. Robert Mulholland, *Shaped by the Word* (Nashville: The Upper Room, 1985), p. 42.
17. *The Book of Discipline, 1988*, p. 81.
18. Mulholland, *Shaped by the Word*, pp. 63-64.
19. Norman Perrin, *The Kingdom of God in the Teachings of Jesus* (London: SCM Press, 1963), p. 24.
20. Colaw, *Beliefs of a United Methodist Christian*, p. 61.
21. *The Book of Discipline, 1988*, par. 203.
22. Richard Joy, *John Wesley's Awakening* (Nashville: The Methodist Church, 1937), p. 116.

Chapter 5   Does the Local Church Have a Role in Our Mission?

1. William H. Willimon and Robert L. Wilson, *Rekindling the Flame* (Nashville: Abingdon Press, 1987), pp. 126-27.
2. Douglas W. Johnson and Alan K. Waltz, *Facts and Possibilities* (Nashville: Abingdon Press, 1987), p. 81.
3. Earl G. Hunt, Jr., *A Bishop Speaks His Mind* (Nashville: Abingdon Press, 1987), p. 155.
4. Johnson and Waltz, *Facts and Possibilities*, p. 129.
5. Ibid., pp. 129-30.
6. James W. Holsinger, Jr., "Developing Lay Spirituality," in *Notes for Lay Leaders* (Nashville: General Board of Discipleship, 1988), p. 1.

7. Ibid.
8. Cynthia B. Astle, "Six 'Spiritual Concerns' Undergirded Lay Project," *The United Methodist Reporter*, June 24, 1988, p. 1.
9. Johnson and Waltz, *Facts and Possibilities*, p. 83.
10. Hunt, *A Bishop Speaks His Mind*, pp. 155-56.
11. Ibid., pp. 156-57.
12. Robert L. Wilson, *Shaping the Congregation* (Nashville: Abingdon Press, 1981), pp. 22-23.
13. Robert L. Wilson and Steve Harper, *Faith and Form* (Grand Rapids, Mich.: Francis Asbury Press, 1988), p. 73.
14. Ibid.
15. Wilson, *Shaping the Congregation*, pp. 26-27.
16. Hunt, *A Bishop Speaks His Mind*, p. 168.
17. Johnson and Waltz, *Facts and Possibilities*, p. 129.
18. Virginia Annual Conference Brochure.
19. Wilson and Harper, *Faith and Form*, p. 119.
20. Johnson and Waltz, *Facts and Possibilities*, p. 84.
21. Alan K. Waltz, *Images of the Future* (Nashville: Abingdon Press, 1980), p. 36.
22. Johnson and Waltz, *Facts and Possibilities*, p. 83.
23. Ibid., p. 84.
24. Johnson and Waltz, *Facts and Possibilities*, p. 138.
25. Willimon and Wilson, *Rekindling the Flame*, p. 123.
26. Richard B. Wilke, *And Are We Yet Alive?* (Nashville: Abingdon Press, 1986), p. 39.
27. Hunt, *A Bishop Speaks His Mind*, p. 46.
28. Willimon and Wilson, *Rekindling the Flame*, p. 96.

Chapter 6　Are We a National Church?

1. John M. Moore, *The Long Road to Methodist Union* (Nashville: The Methodist Publishing House, 1943), p. 32.
2. Ibid., p. 33.
3. *1987 General Minutes of the Annual Conferences of The United Methodist Church* (Evanston, Ill.: General Council on Finance and Administration, 1987).
4. Robert L. Wilson and William H. Willimon, *The Seven Churches of Methodism* (Durham, N. C.: J. M. Ormond Center for Research, Planning and Development, The Divinity School, Duke University, 1985), p. 1.
5. Ibid., pp. 1-2.
6. *The Book of Discipline of The United Methodist Church, 1988* (Nashville: The United Methodist Publishing House, 1988), par. 612.
7. Warren J. Hartman, "Confessions of Faith," *Discipleship Trends*, 3:3, June 1985, p. 1.

8. Ibid., p. 2.
9. Douglas F. Cannon, "Homosexuality Ranked Top Issue," *The United Methodist Reporter*, November 13, 1987, p. 1.
10. Douglas F. Cannon, "Delegates to General Conference Say Leave Sexuality Language Alone," *The United Methodist Reporter*, March 4, 1988, p. 1.
11. Douglas F. Cannon, "Majority of Delegates Polled Consider Proposed Hymn Book 'Improvement,' " *The United Methodist Reporter*, April 1, 1988, p. 1.
12. *The Houston Declaration*, p. 1.
13. Personal communication from Dr. William H. Hinson.
14. Moore, *The Long Road to Methodist Union*, p. 26.
15. Wilson and Willimon, *The Seven Churches of Methodism*, pp. 2-3.
16. Ibid., p. 4.
17. Ibid., p. 6.
18. Ibid., p. 7.
19. Ibid., p. 9.
20. Moore, *The Long Road to Methodist Union*, p. 226.
21. Wilson and Willimon, *The Seven Churches of Methodism*, p. 13.
22. Ibid., p. 17.
23. Ibid., pp. 17-18.
24. Ibid., pp. 18-19.
25. Ibid., p. 19.
26. Ibid. p. 20.
27. *Daily Christian Advocate*, Round-up ed., p. 6.
28. *1987 General Minutes*.

Chapter 7   Where's the CEO?

1. *The Book of Discipline of The United Methodist Church, 1988* (Nashville: The United Methodist Publishing House, 1988), par. 1004.
2. Ibid., par. 50.
3. Terrence E. Deal and Allen A. Kennedy, *Corporate Cultures* (Reading, Mass.: Addison-Wesley Publishing, 1982), pp. 37-38.
4. James McGregor Burns, *Leadership* (New York: Harper & Row, 1978), pp. 451-57.
5. Ira Gallaway, *Drifted Astray* (Nashville: Abingdon Press, 1983), pp. 94, 95.
6. William H. Willimon and Robert L. Wilson, *Rekindling the Flame* (Nashville: Abingdon Press, 1987), p. 60.
7. Ibid., p. 62.
8. Alan K. Waltz, *Images of the Future* (Nashville: Abingdon Press, 1980), p. 49.

9. Richard B. Wilke, *And Are We Yet Alive?* (Nashville: Abingdon Press, 1986), pp. 63-64.
10. Waltz, *Images of the Future*, p. 55.
11. R. Sheldon Duecker, *Tensions in the Connection* (Nashville: Abingdon Press, 1983), p. 54.
12. Ibid., pp. 76-77.
13. Robert L. Wilson and Steve Harper, *Faith and Form* (Grand Rapids, Mich.: Francis Asbury Press, 1988), pp. 134-35.
14. *The Book of Discipline*, par. 527.
15. Duecker, *Tensions in the Connection*, p. 84.
16. Ibid., p. 90.
17. Wilson and Harper, *Faith and Form*, p. 141.
18. *The Book of Discipline*, par. 1004.
19. Douglas W. Johnson and Alan K. Waltz, *Facts and Possibilities* (Nashville: Abingdon Press, 1987), p. 55.
20. Ibid., p. 57.
21. Earl G. Hunt, Jr., *A Bishop Speaks His Mind* (Nashville: Abingdon Press, 1987), p. 141.
22. "Executive Committee Calls for General Boycott of Table Grapes," *The United Methodist Newscope*, July 8, 1988, pp. 1-2.
23. *Daily Christian Advocate*, Round-up ed., p. 10.
24. "Grape Boycott Decision Should Be Rescinded," editorial, *The United Methodist Reporter*, July 8, 1988, p. 2.
25. Wilke, *And Are We Yet Alive?* p. 47.
26. Ibid., p. 59.
27. Ibid.

Chapter 8   Can the Giant Awaken?

1. Richard B. Wilke, *And Are We Yet Alive?* (Nashville: Abingdon Press, 1986), p. 122.
2. Earl G. Hunt, Jr., *A Bishop Speaks His Mind* (Nashville: Abingdon Press, 1987), pp. 60-61.
3. Robert L. Wilson, *Shaping the Congregation* (Nashville: Abingdon Press, 1981), p. 89.
4. Douglas W. Johnson and Alan K. Waltz, *Facts and Possibilities* (Nashville: Abingdon Press, 1987), p. 146.
5. Ibid., p. 147.
6. R. Sheldon Duecker, *Tensions in the Connection* (Nashville: Abingdon Press, 1983), p. 93.

7. *Doctrines and Discipline of The Methodist Church, 1940* (Nashville: The Methodist Publishing House, 1940), p. 184.
8. *The Book of Discipline of The United Methodist Church, 1988* (Nashville: The United Methodist Publishing House, 1988), pp. 145-46.
9. Wilson, *Shaping the Congregation*, p. 89.
10. Hunt, *A Bishop Speaks His Mind*, p. 56.
11. Ibid., p. 57.
12. Johnson and Waltz, *Facts and Possibilities*, p. 147.
13. Ibid., pp. 147-48.
14. Duecker, *Tensions in the Connection*, p. 94.
15. William H. Willimon and Robert L. Wilson, *Rekindling the Flame* (Nashville: Abingdon Press, 1987), p. 104.
16. Wilson, *Shaping the Congregation*, p. 83.
17. Hunt, *A Bishop Speaks His Mind*, p. 57.
18. Alan K. Waltz, *Images of the Future* (Nashville: Abingdon Press, 1980), p. 37.
19. Hunt, *A Bishop Speaks His Mind*, p. 53.
20. James D. Anderson and Ezra Earl Jones, *Ministry of the Laity* (New York: Harper & Row, 1986), front flap.
21. Ibid., p. 25.
22. Christopher Alexander, *The Timeless Way of Building* (New York: Oxford University Press, 1979), p. 41.
23. Anderson and Jones, *Ministry of the Laity*, p. 106.
24. Ibid., p. 107.
25. Ibid., p. 133.
26. Wilke, *And Are We Yet Alive?* p. 122.

Chapter 9   A Lay Prescription for The United Methodist Church?

1. Gus Gustafson, *"I Was . . . Called to Be a Layman"* (Nashville: Abingdon Press, 1982).
2. Robert L. Wilson, *Shaping the Congregation* (Nashville: Abingdon Press, 1981), p. 87.

Index of Scripture

Index of Persons

Index of Titles

Index of Subjects

Index

Index

Printed in the United States
4906